ABOUT THE AUTHOR:

ALINA RIVILIS IS A DATA AND ANALYTICS PROFESSIONAL, A DEVOTED PARENT OF THREE, AND AN AVID ILLUSTRATOR AND COMIC ENTHUSIAST. HER PASSION FOR CREATING ART AND ILLUSTRATING CHILDREN'S BOOKS LED HER TO WRITE THIS BOOK, INSPIRED BY HER OWN CHILDREN. WITH HER UNIQUE BLEND OF ART AND SCIENCE, ALINA PROVIDES A COMPREHENSIVE GUIDE TO HELP CHILDREN AND TEENS CREATE THEIR OWN COMICS AND GRAPHIC NOVELS. JOIN ALINA ON A JOURNEY OF CREATIVITY AND BRING YOUR IMAGINATION TO LIFE ON THE PAGES OF YOUR VERY OWN COMIC BOOK!

MAKE YOUR OWN COMICS:
A GUIDE FOR YOUNG ARTISTS

ALINA RIVILIS

Copyright @ Alina Rivilis, 2023
All Rights Reserved. No part of this publication may be reproduced, stored in a retrieval system, or transmitted, in any form or in any means – by electronic, mechanical, photocopying, recording or otherwise – without prior written permission.

MAKE YOUR OWN COMICS: A GUIDE FOR YOUNG ARTISTS

THIS BOOK IS A PERFECT TOOL FOR STUDENTS, ASPIRING GRAPHIC NOVELISTS, AND THOSE WHO JUST WANT TO START MAKING THEIR OWN COMICS.

ANYONE CAN LEARN HOW TO MAKE COMICS AND GRAPHIC NOVELS. ARE YOU A STUDENT? TEACHER WHO WANTS A PERFECT TEACHING AID TO SPARK CREATIVITY? PARENT WHO WANTS TO INTRODUCE A CHILD TO THE ART OF GRAPHIC NOVEL DESIGN?

LOOK NO FURTHER THAN "MAKE YOUR OWN COMICS: A GUIDE FOR YOUNG ARTISTS".

- 80+ PAGES OF VALUABLE INSTRUCTIONS
- IDEAS AND TEMPLATES TO MAKE YOUR OWN COMIC
- EVERYTHING YOU NEED TO KNOW ABOUT COMIC-MAKING BASICS
- CHARACTER DESIGN
- HEROES, VILLAINS, AND SIDEKICKS
- SPEECH BUBBLES AND SOUND EFFECTS
- SHAPE LANGUAGE
- STORYBOARD AND STORY DEVELOPMENT
- TIPS FOR MAKING AN AWESOME COMIC BOOK

TO UNLEASH YOUR CREATIVITY YOU JUST NEED:

SOME PENCILS AND PENS + PAPER, TEMPLATES AND BLANK PANELS PAGES INCLUDED IN THIS BOOK + YOUR CREATIVITY

DID YOU KNOW?

LEARNING TO MAKE COMIC BOOKS HELPS DEVELOP:

- CREATIVITY
- STORYTELLING SKILLS
- ARTISTIC SKILLS
- READING AND WRITING SKILLS
- SELF-EXPRESSION
- COLLABORATION
- PROBLEM SOLVING SKILLS

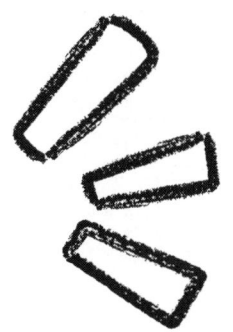

MAKING IT A FUN AND ENGAGING WAY TO LEARN AND EXPRESS YOURSELF.

DO YOU WANT TO MAKE YOUR OWN COMICS?

IF YOU ANSWERED YES, YOU MIGHT HAVE SOME QUESTIONS:

- HOW DO I START?
- DO I NEED TO LEARN HOW TO DRAW?
- WHAT IF I DON'T KNOW HOW TO DRAW?
- HOW TO COME UP WITH INTERESTING CHARACTERS?
- WHAT SHOULD BE THE STORY?
- HOW TO DEVELOP AN INTERESTING PLOT? HOW WOULD MY STORY START AND END?

YOU MIGHT HAVE MANY MORE QUESTIONS... AND IN THIS BOOK, YOU WOULD FIND EASY TO FOLLOW TEMPLATES AND IDEAS TO HELP YOU MAKE AN AWESOME COMIC BOOK!

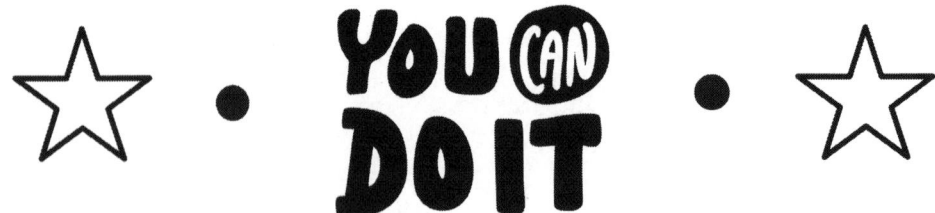

I LOVE READING COMICS AND GRAPHIC NOVELS.
CAN I MAKE MY OWN COMIC?
IS IT DIFFICULT TO MAKE MY OWN COMIC BOOK?
YOU CAN DO IT! IN THIS BOOK YOU WILL FIND LOTS OF TIPS TO MAKE YOUR OWN COMIC BOOK.

TIPS FOR AN AMAZING COMIC BOOK!

- DECIDE ON YOUR MAIN CHARACTER, IS IT A HERO? VILLAIN? A FUNNY SIDEKICK?
- WHERE WILL YOUR STORY TAKE PLACE? JUNGLE? OUTER SPACE? DOWNTOWN?
- WHAT WILL HAPPEN IN YOUR STORY? WOULD A SUPERHERO SAVE THE DAY? WHAT MYSTERY NEEDS TO BE SOLVED?
- USE REALLY COOL PICTURES TO SHOW WHAT'S HAPPENING IN YOUR STORY, AND ADD SPEECH BUBBLES.
- MAKE SURE YOUR STORY FLOWS AND EACH PICTURE SHOWS WHAT'S HAPPENING NEXT.

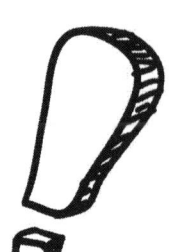

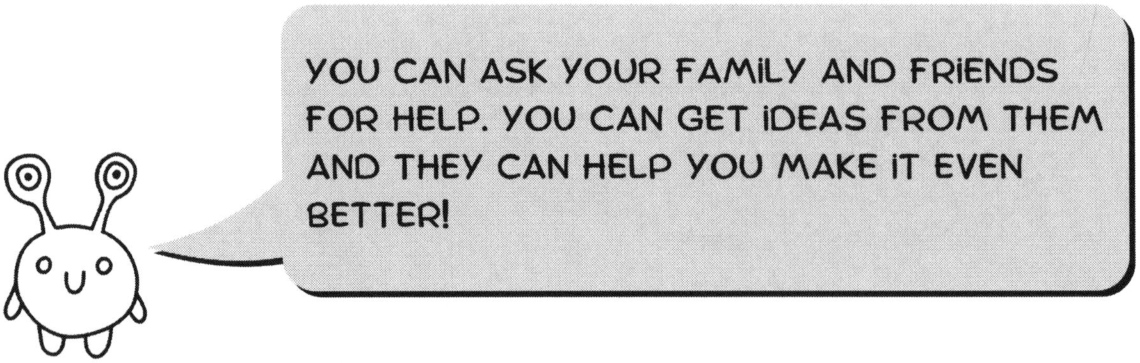

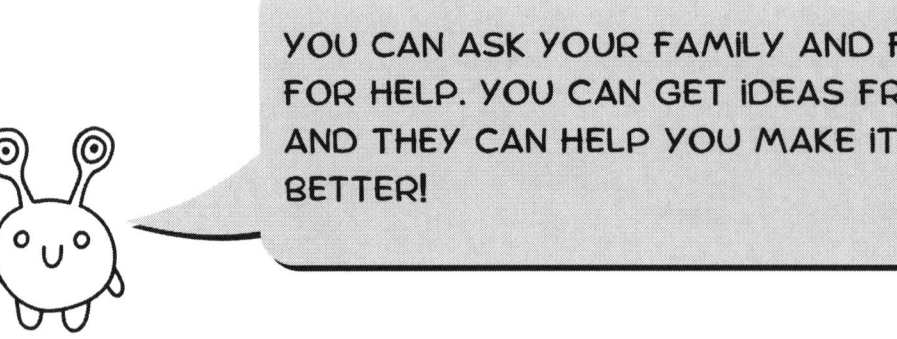

YOU CAN ASK YOUR FAMILY AND FRIENDS FOR HELP. YOU CAN GET IDEAS FROM THEM AND THEY CAN HELP YOU MAKE IT EVEN BETTER!

TO CREATE YOUR COMIC, YOU WOULD NEED TO DECIDE ON:

1. LAYOUT
2. DRAWING STYLE
3. CHOICE OF COLOR
4. CHARACTERS
5. SETTING
6. STORY (EVENTS)

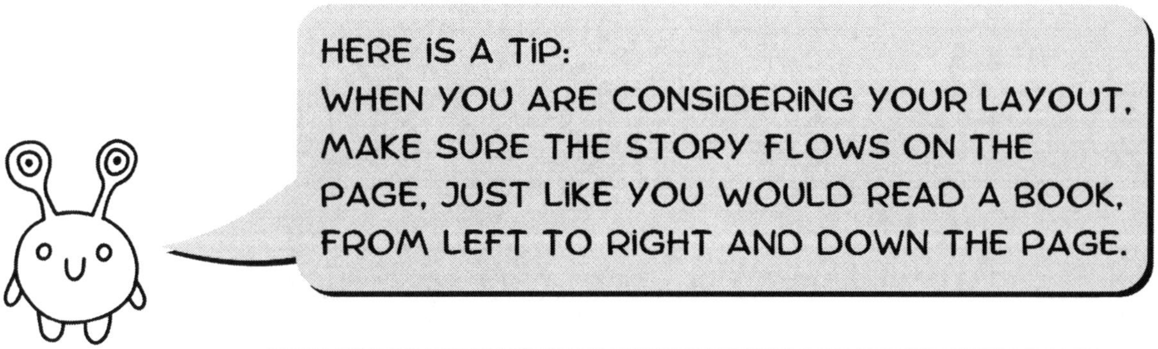

HERE IS A TIP:
WHEN YOU ARE CONSIDERING YOUR LAYOUT, MAKE SURE THE STORY FLOWS ON THE PAGE, JUST LIKE YOU WOULD READ A BOOK, FROM LEFT TO RIGHT AND DOWN THE PAGE.

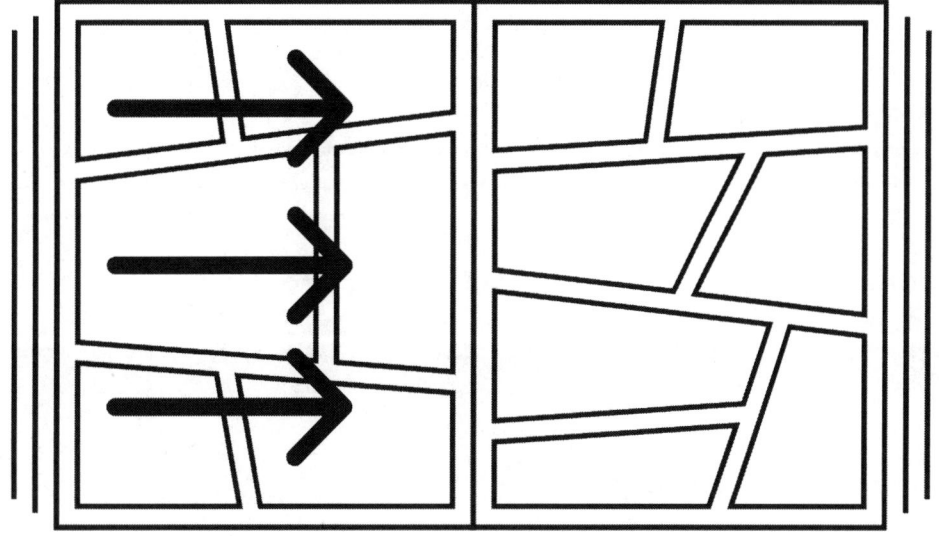

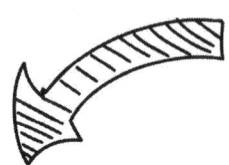

THESE ARE CAPTIONS. THESE ARE VERY USEFUL TO PROVIDE THE NARRATION FOR YOUR STORY AND DESCRIBE THE SCENE OR SETTING.

THESE ARE SPEECH BUBBLES THAT CAPTURE THE DIALOGUE BETWEEN YOUR CHARACTERS (ANYTHING YOUR CHARACTERS SAY OUT-LOUD WOULD BE IN A SPEECH BUBBLE).

ONE SUNNY MORNING, A COUPLE OF ALIENS MET AND HAD A FRIENDLY CHAT...

HI, I AM SPIKEY! WHAT IS YOUR NAME?

HEY, HOW IS IT GOING? I AM DAVE.

CHOOSE A UNIQUE NAME FOR YOUR CHARACTER. ONE OF THE FIRST THINGS THAT READERS WILL NOTICE IS YOUR CHARACTER'S NAME. IT IS IMPORTANT TO CHOOSE A NAME THAT IS MEMORABLE. PERHAPS CONSIDER USING AN ALLITERATION (LIKE "PETER PARKER" OR "BRUCE BANNER") TO MAKE THE NAME STAND OUT.

CRAFTING A CHARACTER'S BACKSTORY HELPS ENHANCE THE CONNECTION WITH THE READER.
- A CHARACTER'S BACKSTORY IS ESSENTIAL FOR SHAPING THEIR IDENTITY.
- CONSIDER THEIR ORIGINS, FAMILY BACKGROUND, AND ANY LIFE-ALTERING EXPERIENCES THAT HAVE OCCURRED.
- THE BACKSTORY HELPS THE READERS TO BETTER RELATE TO THE CHARACTER, MAKING FOR A MORE INTERESTING STORY.

SOUND EFFECTS ARE WORDS WITHOUT BUBBLES THAT MIMIC SOUNDS. THEY ARE NON-VOCAL SOUND IMAGES. THESE CAN BE SOFT, LIKE "HEY", OR LOUD, LIKE "WHAM" FOR AN EXTRA IMPACT. HERE ARE SOME EXAMPLES:

ALL ABOUT PANELS:

- DID YOU KNOW THAT PAGES WITH FEWER PANELS CAN CREATE A SLOWER PACE AND ALLOW FOR MORE DETAILED ARTWORK?
- HOWEVER, PAGES WITH MORE PANELS HAVE A FASTER PACE.
- A "SPLASH PAGE" HAS JUST A SINGLE LARGE PANEL ON A PAGE. IT CAN HELP DRAW THE READER'S ATTENTION.
- VARYING PANEL SIZES AND LAYOUTS CAN ADD VISUAL INTEREST, HERE IS AN EXAMPLE:

LARGE, WIDE PANELS MOVE SLOWER. THEY MIGHT SHOW MULTIPLE CHARACTERS TALKING OR INTERACTING.

SMALLER PANELS ARE "QUICKER", THEY MOVE FASTER FOR THE READER. THESE PANELS MIGHT SHOW A SEQUENCE. THEY OFTEN TEND TO SHOW A SINGLE CHARACTER AND LESS TEXT (OFTEN JUST ONE WORD).

START WITH IDEAS FOR YOUR STORY. THINK ABOUT THE STYLE, SETTING, AND CHARACTERS YOU WANT TO INCLUDE. CONSIDER WHAT YOU WANT TO SAY OR CONVEY THROUGH YOUR STORY.

CONCEPT
PLAN OUT YOUR COMIC BOOK IDEA. WHAT IS YOUR STORY ABOUT? HOW DOES IT START AND END? WHAT HAPPENS IN THE STORY?

CHARACTERS
CREATE FUN CHARACTERS THAT READERS WILL CARE ABOUT AND WOULD WANT TO FOLLOW ALONG.

STORY
WRITE OUT YOUR STORY. YOU SHOULD INCLUDE DESCRIPTIONS OF THE ACTION AND FOCUS ON YOUR PLOT AND CHARACTERS.

STORYBOARD

STORYBOARD YOUR BOOK PANELS. THIS IS A MOCK-UP VERSION OF YOUR ACTUAL COMIC. THINK ABOUT HOW YOUR STORY WOULD FLOW AND WHAT YOU WANT TO SHOW IN YOUR PANELS. WHAT WOULD YOU DRAW? SAY?

ART AND TEXT
AFTER YOU HAVE YOUR STORY IDEA, YOU CAN START WORKING ON YOUR ARTWORK. FINALLY, ADD THE TEXT AND CAPTIONS TO YOUR COMIC.

STEP 1: CHARACTER
Decide on your characters. Who are the heroes? Is there a villain? A sidekick?

STEP 2: SETTING
Where does your story take place? Space? Haunted house? School? In the city?

STEP 3: EVENT
What happens in the story? A mystery? A problem? Who will solve it? How?

WOW!

Write your words in bubbles like this one and make sure the bubble points to your character's head

STEP 4: DRAW!
Sketch your ideas in pencil first, and add color next (you can use markers and crayons). Don't forget to add some action words to make it POP!

STEP 5: TEXT BUBBLES
Write your words and draw "bubbles" around to tell your story.

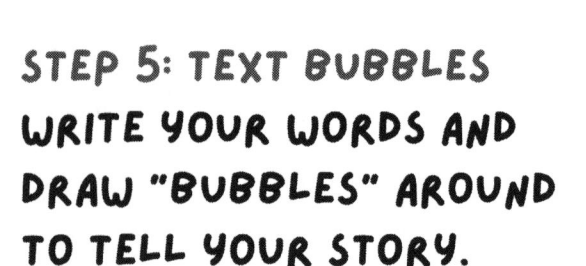

EVERY COMIC NEEDS A MAIN CHARACTER.

A CENTRAL **HERO** OR **VILLAIN** WOULD MAKE FOR A FUN AND INTERESTING STORY.

START BY CREATING YOUR MAIN CHARACTER:

- WHAT SHE OR HE WOULD LOOK LIKE?
- WHAT IS THEIR STYLE? VOICE? PERSONALITY?
- WHAT MAKES THE CHARACTER INTERESTING?
- DOES THE CHARACTER HAVE A STORY? A GOAL OR MISSION?
- WHAT WOULD BE THEIR POWERS AND WEAKNESSES OR STRUGGLES (THIS MAKES YOUR STORY MORE INTERESTING).
- DOES YOUR CHARACTER HAVE AN ENEMY? ADDING A VILLAIN ALSO MAKES FOR A FUN AND DYNAMIC STORY.

GET INSPIRED! THINK ABOUT POPULAR CHARACTERS IN COMICS, MOVIES AND SHOWS. WHAT MAKES THEM INTERESTING? POPULAR?

AN INTERESTING CHARACTER DOESN'T HAVE TO BE A SUPER HERO. YOU CAN ALWAYS ASK YOUR FAMILY AND FRIENDS FOR IDEAS.

HEROES, VILLAINS AND SIDEKICKS

ARE YOU GOING TO HAVE A HERO? A VILLAIN? PERHAPS A SIDEKICK IN YOUR STORY?

- WHAT DOES YOUR MAIN CHARACTER WANT OR NEED? IS YOUR MAIN CHARACTER A HERO OR A VILLAIN?
- WHAT ARE THEIR STRENGTHS? WEAKNESSES?
- WHO ARE THE OTHER CHARACTERS IN YOUR STORY?
- WHAT IS THE ROLE OF THE SUPPORTING CHARACTERS?

"ONE-EYE"

POWERS:
- SUPER EYE
- EXTRA FRIENDLY
- MAGIC (NEEDS A SMILE TO ACTIVATE)

WEAKNESS:
- LOUD NOISES AND ANGER

ENEMY:
- ANGER MONSTER

"ANGER MONSTER"

STRENGTHS:
- LOUD NOISES AND ANGER

ENEMY:
- ONE-EYE

HERO:
〜〜〜〜〜〜〜〜〜〜〜〜〜〜〜〜〜

WHAT MAKES HEROES AMAZING? WHY DO WE LOVE SPIDER-MAN, BATMAN, SUPERMAN, WONDER WOMAN, AND CAPTAIN AMERICA? DO YOU HAVE A FAVORITE COMIC BOOK HERO?

APPEARANCE AND NAME:
THE MAIN HERO SHOULD HAVE A DISTINCT LOOK AND NAME. YOUR HERO SHOULD BE EASY TO TELL APART FROM OTHER CHARACTERS.
- THINK ABOUT SPIDER-MAN'S RED AND BLUE SUIT, HE REALLY STANDS OUT!

MOTIVATION:
THE MAIN HERO SHOULD HAVE A REASON FOR FIGHTING OR TAKING ACTION. HEROES OFTEN WANT TO HELP OTHERS OR NEED TO FIGHT FOR JUSTICE. WHAT MOTIVATES YOUR HERO?
- BATMAN IS DRIVEN BY A DESIRE TO AVENGE HIS PARENTS' DEATHS AND PROTECT GOTHAM CITY.

FLAWS AND WEAKNESSES:
YOUR MAIN HERO SHOULD NOT BE PERFECT, AS THIS CAN MAKE THEM BORING OR UNRELATABLE. CONSIDER GIVING THEM A FLAW OF A WEAKNESS THAT THEY NEED TO OVERCOME IN ORDER TO SUCCEED.
- SUPERMAN'S WEAKNESS TO KRYPTONITE ADDS AN INTERESTING TWIST AND GIVES VULNERABILITY TO HIS CHARACTER.

HUMOR, QUIRKS AND ANTICS:
HUMOR CAN MAKE A MAIN HERO MORE LIKABLE AND HELP BALANCE OUT SERIOUS OR DRAMATIC MOMENTS.
- DEADPOOL'S SARCASM ADD HUMOR TO HIS VIOLENT AND ACTION-PACKED STORIES.
- SPIDERMAN IS OFTEN FUNNY AND QUIRKY WITH HIS COMMENTS.

> WHAT ARE SOME TRAITS THAT MAKE UP A HERO? PICK A HEROIC CHARACTER AND THINK ABOUT THEIR TRAITS. HOW DO THEY SHOW THESE TRAITS? WHAT MAKES THESE TRAITS HEROIC? IS THE HERO ALWAYS "GOOD"?

HERE IS A TIP:
ONCE YOU HAVE CREATED YOUR MAIN CHARACTER, YOU CAN FOLLOW THE SAME APPROACH TO CREATE WELL-ROUNDED SUPPORTING CHARACTERS AND VILLAINS.

OFTEN A HERO HAS A SECRET!

FOR EXAMPLE, A SECRET IDENTITY. THE HERO HAS DIFFERENT CHALLENGES WHEN SHE IS IN HER SUPERHERO FORM, AND MUST FACE A DIFFERENT SET OF CHALLENGES IN HER EVERY-DAY, REGULAR LIFE.

WHO IS OUR HERO?
WHAT POWERS DO THEY HAVE?
WHAT IS THEIR NAME?
WHAT IS THEIR MISSION?
HOW DO THEY DO IT?
DO THEY HAVE A SECRET IDENTITY?
IF YOU COULD BE A HERO, WHAT POWERS WOULD YOU HAVE?

VILLAIN:

GOAL OR MOTIVE:
A GOOD VILLAIN SHOULD HAVE A CLEAR MOTIVE FOR THEIR ACTIONS. IT MIGHT BE A DESIRE FOR POWER, REVENGE, OR SOMETHING ELSE ENTIRELY.
- MAGNETO'S GOAL IS CREATING A SEPARATE SOCIETY FOR MUTANTS

PERSONALITY:
A DISTINCT PERSONALITY MAKES FOR AN INTERESTING ENEMY. IT SHOULD SET THEM APART FROM OTHER CHARACTERS IN THE STORY. THEY SHOULD BE MEMORABLE AND INTERESTING.
- JOKER'S CHAOTIC AND UNPREDICTABLE NATURE MAKES HIM INTERESTING

A WORTHY OPPONENT:
THE VILLAIN SHOULD POSE A REAL THREAT TO THE MAIN HERO, IT COULD BE USING THEIR PHYSICAL ABILITIES OR THEIR INTELLECT. THE VILLAIN POSES A CHALLENGE TO THE HERO AND KEEPS THE READER INTERESTED IN THE STORY.
- THE INTELLIGENCE AND WEALTH OF LEX LUTHOR MAKE HIM A STRONG OPPONENT FOR SUPERMAN

HUMAN AND SYMPATHETIC QUALITIES:
A GOOD VILLAIN SHOULD HAVE SOME SYMPATHETIC QUALITIES OR A BACKSTORY. WHY DID THEY TURN TO EVIL?? THIS CAN ADD DEPTH TO THEIR CHARACTER.
- CATWOMAN'S BACKGROUND AND HER COMPLICATED RELATIONSHIP WITH BATMAN ADD COMPLEXITY TO THE STORY.

WHAT MAKES MAGNETO, THE JOKER, AND LEX LUTHOR INTERESTING?

WHAT DO YOU THINK ABOUT CHARACTERS LIKE DOCTOR DOOM AND CATWOMAN? CAN YOU THINK OF OTHER VILLAINS AND WHAT MAKES THEM A CHALLENGE TO THE MAIN CHARACTER?

SIDEKICK:
∿∿∿∿∿∿∿∿∿∿∿

WHY DO SOME HEROES HAVE A PAL WHO HELPS THEM OUT? WHAT MAKES A SIDEKICK INTERESTING? WHY DOES BATMAN HAVE A ROBIN TO HELP HIM OUT??

SKILLS THAT ARE A COMPLEMENT: THE SIDEKICK CHARACTER TENDS TO SUPPORT THE MAIN CHARACTER, AND OFTEN HAS SKILLS THAT ARE COMPLEMENTARY TO THE MAIN CHARACTER. A GOOD SIDEKICK SHOULD COMPLEMENT THE HERO'S STRENGTHS OR WEAKNESSES. THIS CAN MAKE THEM A VALUABLE PARTNER IN BATTLE OR IN SOLVING PROBLEMS.
- ROBIN'S ACROBATIC SKILLS AND QUICK THINKING MAKE HIM A VALUABLE ALLY TO BATMAN.

DISTINCT PERSONALITY: A SIDEKICK SHOULD HAVE A DISTINCT PERSONALITY THAT SETS THEM APART FROM THE MAIN HERO. THEY SHOULD BE MEMORABLE AND INTERESTING TO READ ABOUT.
- CHEWBACCA'S LOYALTY AND FIERCE PROTECTIVENESS MAKE HIM A GREAT SIDEKICK TO HAN SOLO. DON'T YOU JUST LOVE THE LOOK OF THIS CHARACTER? CHEWBACCA REALLY STANDS OUT FROM ALL OTHER CHARACTERS.

SENSE OF HUMOR: LIKE THE MAIN HERO, A SIDEKICK WITH A SENSE OF HUMOR CAN PROVIDE COMIC RELIEF TO SERIOUS OR DRAMATIC SITUATIONS.
- RON WEASLEY'S HUMOROUS QUIPS AND LOYALTY MAKE HIM A BELOVED SIDEKICK TO HARRY POTTER.

ROOM FOR GROWTH: A GOOD SIDEKICK SHOULD HAVE ROOM FOR DEVELOPMENT, EITHER THROUGH LEARNING NEW SKILLS OR OVERCOMING CHALLENGES.
- BUCKY BARNES' JOURNEY FROM SIDEKICK TO INDEPENDENT HERO IN THE CAPTAIN AMERICA COMICS ADDS DEPTH TO HIS CHARACTER.

HAVE YOU GOT A FAVORITE SIDEKICK?
DO YOU LIKE ROBIN?
WHAT DO YOU THINK ABOUT CHEWBACCA?
HOW ABOUT HERMIONE GRANGER OR BUCKY BARNES? ARE ANY OTHER SIDEKICKS COME TO MIND?

SUPER POWERS!!!

SUPERPOWERS ARE OFTEN WHAT MAKE COMIC BOOK CHARACTERS STAND OUT. THINK ABOUT WHAT KIND OF POWER OR ABILITY YOUR CHARACTER MIGHT HAVE, AND HOW IT MIGHT BE USEFUL IN THE STORY. YOU CAN ALSO CONSIDER GIVING THEM A UNIQUE SKILL OR TALENT THAT SETS THEM APART FROM OTHER CHARACTERS.

EVEN IF YOUR CHARACTER HAS SUPERPOWERS OR A UNIQUE PERSONALITY, IT'S IMPORTANT TO MAKE THEM RELATABLE TO READERS.

WHEN DESIGNING YOUR CHARACTER:
- WHAT CHALLENGES THEY MIGHT FACE?
- HOW THEY MIGHT OVERCOME THEM?
- DO THEY HAVE FLAWS OR INSECURITIES?
- WHAT MAKES THEM RELATABLE?

FLAWS AND CHALLENGES CAN MAKE YOUR CHARACTER MORE HUMAN.

I have GIRL POWER! I can turn my dreams into reality. I believe in myself and can make anything happen!

HERE ARE SOME ADJECTIVES TO HELP WITH CHARACTER DESIGN:

PERSONALITY TRAITS:
- BRAVE, FUNNY, MYSTERIOUS, KIND-HEARTED, ADVENTUROUS, INTELLIGENT, MISCHIEVOUS, COMPASSIONATE, DETERMINED, LOYAL, QUICK-WITTED, OPTIMISTIC, CHARISMATIC, RESILIENT, GENTLE, THOUGHTFUL, CONFIDENT, HUMBLE, AMBITIOUS.

PHYSICAL DESCRIPTIONS:
- TALL, SHORT, MUSCULAR, SLIM, CURVY, ATHLETIC, WIRY, PETITE, ELEGANT, GRACEFUL, RUGGED, CHARMING, QUIRKY, EXPRESSIVE, STRIKING, FIERCE, SCRUFFY, DAINTY, IMPOSING, ENCHANTING.

EMOTIONAL STATES:
- HAPPY, SAD, EXCITED, ANGRY, SCARED, CURIOUS, CALM, SURPRISED, BORED, CONTENT, ANXIOUS, CONFIDENT, PROUD, EMBARRASSED, JEALOUS, DETERMINED, OPTIMISTIC, SKEPTICAL, INTRIGUED, OVERWHELMED.

ABILITIES AND POWERS:
- SUPER STRENGTH, SPEED, INVISIBILITY, SHAPE-SHIFTING, TELEPATHY, TELEPORTATION, ELEMENTAL CONTROL, TIME MANIPULATION, MIND READING, PRECOGNITION, HEALING, ENERGY PROJECTION, TELEKINESIS, SUPER INTELLIGENCE, FLIGHT, HEIGHTENED SENSES, PHASING, ELASTICITY, SUPER AGILITY.

ATTITUDES AND BEHAVIORS:
- CARING, SARCASTIC, IMPULSIVE, ANALYTICAL, REBELLIOUS, SARCASTIC, COMPASSIONATE, QUIRKY, INTROVERTED, EXTROVERTED, MISCHIEVOUS, SELFLESS, STUBBORN, DIPLOMATIC, ASSERTIVE, CAUTIOUS, CREATIVE, METHODICAL, ADAPTABLE, ADVENTUROUS, WITTY, ENIGMATIC.

RELATIONSHIPS AND INTERACTIONS:
- SUPPORTIVE, LOYAL, PROTECTIVE, HUMOROUS, MENTOR, SIBLING, RIVAL, ROMANTIC, ANTAGONIST, PARTNER, TRUSTWORTHY, UNRELIABLE, COMPASSIONATE, ADVERSARIAL, PARENTAL, CONFLICTED, DYNAMIC, FRIENDSHIP, ENVIOUS, MANIPULATIVE, PLATONIC, LOVE-HATE.

> WHAT OTHER ADJECTIVES COME TO MIND??
> IS YOUR MAIN CHARACTER HAPPY? SAD? HOW DO THEY SOLVE THEIR CHALLENGES?
> MIX AND MATCH THESE IDEAS TO DESIGN AN AMAZING CHARACTER!

GIVE YOUR CHARACTER A UNIQUE APPEARANCE

CREATING A COMIC BOOK CHARACTER CAN BE A LOT OF FUN. WHAT YOUR CHARACTER LOOKS LIKE CAN BE JUST AS IMPORTANT AS THEIR PERSONALITY.

- WHAT THEY WEAR?
- HOW DO THEY STYLE THEIR HAIR?
- ANY UNIQUE PHYSICAL FEATURES THEY MIGHT HAVE?
- WHAT MAKES THEM DIFFERENT? UNIQUE?

YOU CAN DRAW A FEW SKETCHES OF YOUR CHARACTER TO HELP YOU VISUALIZE THEM.

YOUR CHARACTER'S PERSONALITY IS WHAT WILL MAKE THEM MEMORABLE TO READERS. THINK ABOUT THEIR LIKES AND DISLIKES, THEIR STRENGTHS AND WEAKNESSES, AND HOW THEY INTERACT WITH OTHER CHARACTERS IN THE STORY.

DID YOU KNOW?

- Batman's arch-nemesis the Joker was originally supposed to be killed off in his first appearance, but the character was so popular that he ended up becoming a recurring villain.

- Spider-Man's web-slinging abilities were inspired by a visit to a science exhibit where creator Stan Lee saw a machine that used streams of water to create a spider-web-like pattern.

- Superman's alter-ego Clark Kent was named after two actors: Clark Gable and Kent Taylor!

- Wolverine's claws are not actually part of his mutant power, but rather are made of bone that he can retract and extend at will.

- Harley Quinn, who started as a sidekick to the Joker, was originally created for the Batman: The Animated Series TV show before being incorporated into the comics.

- Black Panther, who made his first appearance in 1966, was the first Black superhero in mainstream American comics.

- Iron Man's suit was initially designed to keep Tony Stark alive after he was injured in a warzone, but he later upgraded it with weapons and other advanced technology.

- The X-Men's Cyclops, whose real name is Scott Summers, is one of the few characters in the Marvel universe who is known to wear glasses.

- Catwoman who is known for her love-hate relationship with Batman, was originally introduced as a thief and adversary.

- The Teenage Mutant Ninja Turtles, who were created as a parody of popular comics at the time and were named after famous Renaissance artists Leonardo, Michelangelo, Donatello, and Raphael.

CHARACTER DESIGN

THE FOLLOWING ARE IMPORTANT TO CONSIDER WHEN DESIGNING YOUR CHARACTER:

> CREATING A UNIQUE AND COMPELLING CHARACTER IS ALL ABOUT IMAGINATION AND THINKING OUTSIDE THE BOX.

- NAME:
    - AN INTERESTING NAME BRINGS YOUR CHARACTER TO LIFE.
- APPEARANCE:
    - WHAT DOES YOUR CHARACTER LOOK LIKE?
    - HAIRSTYLE, FACIAL FEATURES, BODY TYPE AND CLOTHING?
- SUPERPOWER OR ABILITIES:
    - WHAT UNIQUE POWER OR ABILITIES DO THEY HAVE?
    - WHAT MAKES THEM SPECIAL?
- PERSONALITY TRAITS:
    - WHAT ADJECTIVES DESCRIBE YOUR CHARACTER'S PERSONALITY?
        - BRAVE, SILLY, SMART, FUNNY, OR MYSTERIOUS?
- BACKSTORY:
    - THINK ABOUT YOUR CHARACTER'S BACKGROUND AND THEIR MOTIVATION FOR BECOMING A HERO OR VILLAIN.
- WEAKNESSES:
    - GREAT CHARACTERS HAVE THEIR WEAKNESSES. WHAT ARE THE VULNERABILITIES OF YOUR CHARACTER?
- SIDEKICK OR COMPANION:
    - DESCRIBE THEIR RELATIONSHIP AND HOW THEY HELP EACH OTHER.
- ARCH-NEMESIS:
    - INVENT AN ARCH-NEMESIS FOR YOUR CHARACTER. WHAT MAKES THEM A FORMIDABLE OPPONENT?
- CATCHPHRASE:
    - WHAT IS YOUR CHARACTER'S CATCHPHRASE OR MEMORABLE LINE? WRITE IT DOWN!

DESIGN A CHARACTER:

- NAME YOUR CHARACTER: _____

- WHAT DO THEY LOOK LIKE? _____
_____

- SUPER POWERS? ABILITIES? _____
_____

- PERSONALITY? _____
_____

- CREATE A BACKSTORY FOR YOUR CHARACTER:
_____
_____
_____

- WEAKNESSES: _____

- SIDEKICK: _____

- CREATE A LIST OF ENEMIES OR VILLAINS YOUR HERO FACES:
_____
_____
_____

- CATCHPHRASE: _____
_____

DRAW YOUR CHARACTER:

NAME:

POWERS:
_____
_____
_____

WEAKNESSES:
_____
_____
_____

DRAW THEIR SIDEKICK:
NAME:

DRAW THEIR ENEMY:
NAME:

SETTING

- WHERE DOES THE STORY TAKE PLACE?
- YOU CAN CREATE A WORLD FOR YOUR STORY (IT CAN BE REAL OR FROM YOUR IMAGINATION).
- WHAT MAKES YOUR SETTING OR WORLD SPECIAL OR INTERESTING? ARE THERE FUNNY MONSTERS OR ALIENS WHO LIVE THERE?

HERE IS A TIP:
OFTEN IN COMICS, THE FIRST PAGE SHOWS THE SETTING. YOU WOULD NOTICE THAT THIS SETS THE TONE FOR THE REST OF THE PAGES AND HELPS UNDERSTAND WHERE THE STORY TAKES PLACE.

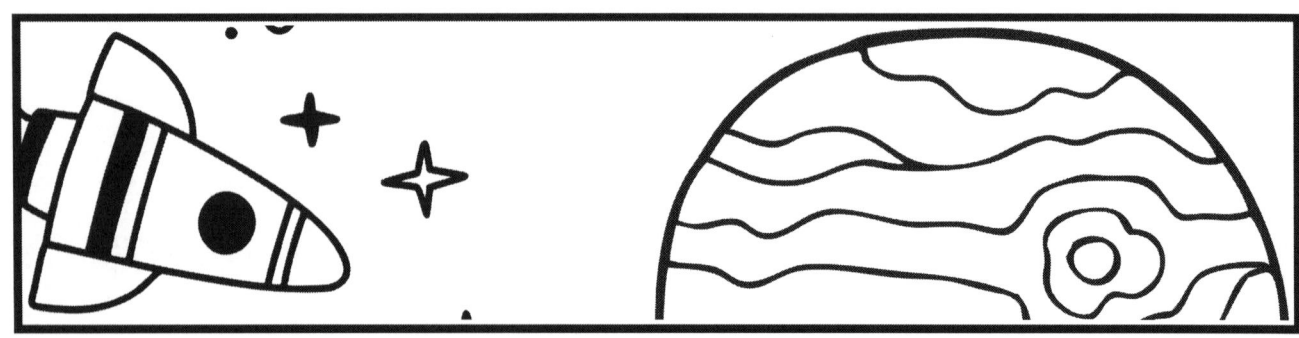

THE "ESTABLISHING SHOT"

THE ESTABLISHING SHOT IS A PANEL THAT OFTEN COMES AT THE BEGINNING OF A SCENE. THIS IS DONE TO TELL THE READER ABOUT THE SETTING. THIS HELPS SET THE MOOD, SHOW WHERE AND WHEN THE SCENE WILL BE TAKING PLACE, AND HELPS THE READER UNDERSTAND THE CHARACTER'S LOCATION.

> THE ESTABLISHING SHOT SETS THE SETTING. EVERY CHAPTER OR SCENE SHOULD HAVE AN ESTABLISHING SHOT TO HELP THE READER UNDERSTAND THE CONTEXT.

WE START OUR STORY WITH SHOWING A SPACE SHIP. THIS ESTABLISHES OUR COMIC STORY AS A SPACE STORY. THE READER UNDERSTANDS THAT THE FOLLOWING PANELS TAKE PLACE IN SPACE.

MORE ABOUT "SHOTS"!

DID YOU KNOW THAT COMIC BOOKS OFTEN USE DIFFERENT TYPES OF SHOTS TO CREATE DYNAMIC AND FUN PANELS. SOME COMMON ONES INCLUDE:

- WIDE SHOT:
    - THIS SHOT PROVIDES AN OVERALL VIEW OF THE SCENE OR SETTING, SHOWING A LARGE AREA OR GROUP OF CHARACTERS. IT HELPS ESTABLISH THE LOCATION AND CONTEXT WITHIN THE STORY.
        - THE TERMS "WIDE SHOT" AND THE "ESTABLISHING SHOT" ARE OFTEN USED INTERCHANGEABLY IN COMIC BOOKS. THEY CAN HAVE SLIGHT DIFFERENCES IN THEIR PURPOSE.
        - BOTH HELP PROVIDE A BROAD VIEW OF THE SCENE OR SETTING, ESTABLISHING THE LOCATION AND CONTEXT WITHIN THE STORY. THEY ARE TYPICALLY USED AT THE BEGINNING OF A NEW SCENE OR TO TRANSITION BETWEEN DIFFERENT LOCATIONS.

THIS IS THE FIRST PANEL, IT USES A WIDE OR "ESTABLISHING" SHOT TO SET THE STORY. WE SEE BOTH OF THE CHARACTERS AT A PARK OR A POND? WE ALSO SEE THAT THESE CHARACTERS MIGHT BE FRIENDS. THIS GIVES THE READER AN IDEA ABOUT THE SETTING AND WHAT MIGHT BE HAPPENING NEXT IN THE STORY.

- **CLOSE-UP SHOT:**
  - A CLOSE-UP SHOT FOCUSES ON A SPECIFIC CHARACTER, OBJECT, OR DETAIL, EMPHASIZING ITS IMPORTANCE OR SIGNIFICANCE. IT CAN BE USED TO CONVEY EMOTIONS, REACTIONS, OR KEY ELEMENTS OF THE STORY.

- **MEDIUM SHOT:**
  - A MEDIUM SHOT FRAMES THE CHARACTER FROM THE WAIST UP, ALLOWING FOR MORE BODY LANGUAGE AND INTERACTION WITH THE SURROUNDINGS. IT PROVIDES A BALANCE BETWEEN SHOWING THE CHARACTER AND THE SURROUNDING ENVIRONMENT.

THIS IS AN EXAMPLE OF A MEDIUM SHOT. THE CHARACTER IS SHOWN FROM THE WAIST UP.

THIS IS AN EXAMPLE OF A CLOSE UP SHOT!

MOTION LINES AND EXAGGERATED POSES

MOTION LINES SHOW MOVEMENT

- **DYNAMIC ACTION SHOTS:**

COMIC BOOKS OFTEN USE DYNAMIC ACTION SHOTS TO DEPICT FAST-PACED SEQUENCES OR INTENSE MOMENTS. THESE CAN INCLUDE DIAGONAL PANELS, MOTION LINES, SPEED LINES, AND EXAGGERATED POSES TO CONVEY MOVEMENT, ENERGY, AND EXCITEMENT.

SPEED LINES

MOTION LINES, OFTEN CALLED ACTION OR SPEED LINES, HELP DEPICT MOVEMENT

MOTION LINES SHOW THAT THE CHARACTER IS RUNNING.

DEVELOP YOUR STORY

CREATING AN INTERESTING COMIC BOOK STORY CAN BE A COMPLEX PROCESS. HERE ARE SOME IDEAS FOR AN AWESOME STORY:

TIPS FOR CRAFTING THE MIDDLE OF YOUR STORY:

- BUILD UPON THE CONFLICT AND CHARACTERS INTRODUCED IN THE BEGINNING
- CREATE TENSION AND INTRODUCE NEW TWISTS AND SUBPLOTS
- ENSURE EACH SCENE MOVES THE STORY FORWARD AND IS RELEVANT TO THE OVERALL PLOT
- CONSIDER BUILDING TOWARDS A MAJOR EVENT FOR THE CHARACTERS TO OVERCOME.

START WITH THE SETTING, INTRODUCE THE CHARACTERS, AND SET UP THE MAIN CONFLICT.
YOU WANT TO GRAB THE READER'S ATTENTION AND MAKE THEM INTERESTED IN THE STORY.

THE END OF A STORY SERVES TO RESOLVE THE CONFLICT AND PROVIDE A CONCLUSION. IT IS IMPORTANT TO LEAVE READERS FEELING SATISFIED WITH THE RESOLUTION, WHILE ALSO SETTING UP A POTENTIAL SEQUEL OR LEAVING ROOM FOR FUTURE STORIES IF YOU PLAN TO CREATE A SERIES.

EVENT

- WHAT PROBLEM WOULD YOUR MAIN CHARACTER FACE?
- WHAT'S STOPPING YOUR HERO OR VILLAIN FROM GETTING WHAT THEY WANT?
- WHAT CHALLENGES WILL YOUR MAIN CHARACTER NEED TO OVERCOME?
- WHAT OBSTACLES WILL THEY FACE ALONG THE WAY?
- WHAT WILL HAPPEN IF YOUR MAIN CHARACTER DOESN'T SOLVE THE PROBLEM? WHAT ARE THE CONSEQUENCES?
- HOW WILL YOUR MAIN CHARACTER SOLVE THE PROBLEM? WHAT WILL THEY NEED TO DO?

> IT IS ESSENTIAL TO HAVE A STRONG NARRATIVE. START BY CONCEPTUALIZING THE BEGINNING, MIDDLE, AND END OF YOUR STORY. IT'S CRUCIAL TO WRITE A SCRIPT BEFORE DRAWING ANYTHING, AS IT PROVIDES DIRECTION AND CLARITY.

ALIEN SPACE STORY:

| GO ON A SPACE ADVENTURE | LAND ON AN ALIEN PLANET | MEET FRIENDLY ALIENS, MAKE NEW FRIENDS |

THERE ARE NO WRONG ANSWERS! HAVE FUN WITH YOUR STORY AND LET YOUR IMAGINATION RUN WILD. THE MORE YOU THINK ABOUT YOUR CHARACTERS, THEIR STORY AND THEIR WORLD, THE MORE INTERESTING YOUR COMIC BOOK WOULD BE.

WHAT STORY DO YOU WANT TO TELL? WHAT IS YOUR COMIC BOOK STORY ABOUT?

WHAT DO YOU WANT YOUR READERS TO LEARN OR FEEL AFTER READING YOUR COMIC BOOK?

WHAT MESSAGE DO YOU WANT TO SHARE IN YOUR STORY?

AN INTERESTING STORY PLOT MAKES FOR AN AWESOME COMIC. CONSIDER ADDING PLOT TWISTS OR UNEXPECTED EVENTS TO KEEP READERS ON THE EDGE OF THEIR SEATS!

LET'S CREATE A STORY!
(EXAMPLE)

LET'S SAY YOUR MAIN CHARACTER IS A SUPERHERO NAMED SUPER CAT WHO LIVES IN A WORLD FULL OF OTHER ANIMALS! SUPER CAT HAS TWO SIDEKICKS, THEY ARE KITTENS WHO HELP SUPER CAT ON HIS MISSION. SUPER CAT NEEDS TO SAVE THE CITY FROM VILLAINS.

SETTING: THE CITY

CHALLENGE: EVIL VILLAINS STOLE ALL THE CATNIP IN THE CITY!!

- WITHOUT CATNIP, SUPER CAT CAN'T USE HIS SUPERPOWERS!! THIS IS A TOTAL DISASTER, WOULDN'T YOU AGREE?

MISSION: SNEAK INTO THE VILLAINS' LAIR, AND GET THAT CATNIP

HOW DOES THE STORY END?
SUPER CAT AND HIS FRIENDS WORK TOGETHER TO DEFEAT THE VILLAINS AND GET ALL THAT STOLEN CATNIP! SUPER CAT IS BACK IN ACTION! CATNIP HELPS SUPER CAT TO USE HIS POWERS AGAIN, AND RESTORE PEACE IN THE CITY.

GO SUPER CAT!

Meow

LET'S CREATE A STORY!
(ANOTHER EXAMPLE USING A SIMPLE TEMPLATE)

CHARACTER	SETTING	EVENT
SUPER CAT	THE PARK	SUPER CAT SAVES THE DAY FROM TRASH!

SUPER CAT SAVES THE DAY FROM TRASH! SHE RECYCLES AND SAVES THE PLANET! PEOPLE KEEP THROWING THEIR GARBAGE ALL OVER THE PLACE, AND THE PARK IS SO DIRTY. SUPER CAT COMES TO THE RESCUE!

MEOW

STORYBOARD

A STORYBOARD IS A PLAN FOR A COMIC BOOK. IT HELPS THE CREATORS TO FIGURE OUT HOW THE STORY WILL LOOK ON THE PAGES BEFORE THEY START DRAWING IT.

THE STORYBOARD IS MADE UP OF MANY LITTLE PICTURES CALLED PANELS THAT SHOW WHAT IS HAPPENING IN THE STORY. THESE SMALL PICTURES AND OFTEN DESCRIPTIONS NEXT TO THE PICTURE TELL A STORY, JUST LIKE A COMIC BOOK.

DID YOU KNOW? CREATORS USE THE STORYBOARD TO DECIDE WHAT HAPPENS IN EACH PANEL, WHAT THE CHARACTERS SAY, AND HOW THEY MOVE FROM ONE PANEL TO THE NEXT. THEY CAN ALSO TRY OUT DIFFERENT WAYS TO ARRANGE THE PANELS TO MAKE THE STORY MORE EXCITING.

- THE STORYBOARD ACTS AS A REFERENCE TO CREATE THE FINAL COMIC BOOK PAGES.
- ONCE THE CREATORS ARE HAPPY WITH THE STORYBOARD, THEY CAN START DRAWING THE COMIC BOOK, USING THE PANELS AND THE PLAN AS A GUIDE TO MAKE SURE THEY DON'T FORGET ANYTHING.

SO, A STORYBOARD IS LIKE A COMIC BOOK'S MAP THAT HELPS THE CREATORS PLAN AND DRAW THE STORY BEFORE IT BECOMES A REAL COMIC BOOK.

WHY SHOULD I MAKE A STORYBOARD?

A STORYBOARD IS A TOOL TO HELP YOU PLAN YOUR COMIC BOOK,

STEPS TO MAKE A STORYBOARD

1. BEGIN WITH A CLEAR IDEA OF THE STORY YOU WANT TO TELL. THIS WILL HELP YOU TO CREATE A STRUCTURE FOR YOUR STORYBOARD.
2. DECIDE ON THE NUMBER OF PANELS THAT YOU WILL NEED FOR YOUR STORY. PANELS ARE THE BOXES WHERE YOU WILL DRAW YOUR IMAGES AND WRITE YOUR TEXT.
3. DRAW ROUGH SKETCHES OF EACH PANEL. YOU DON'T NEED TO MAKE THEM PERFECT, JUST DRAW ENOUGH TO SHOW THE ACTION AND WHAT IS HAPPENING IN EACH PANEL.
4. WRITE DOWN NOTES FOR EACH PANEL TO DESCRIBE WHAT IS HAPPENING IN THE SCENE.
5. ARRANGE THE PANELS IN THE ORDER YOU WANT THEM TO APPEAR IN YOUR STORY. YOU CAN TRY OUT DIFFERENT SEQUENCES UNTIL YOU FIND WHAT WORKS BEST FOR YOUR STORY.
6. ONCE YOU HAVE YOUR PANELS AND NOTES FINALIZED, YOU CAN TRANSFER THEM ONTO A STORYBOARD TEMPLATE OR DRAW THEM ONTO PAPER TO CREATE YOUR FINAL STORYBOARD.
7. REVIEW YOUR STORYBOARD AND MAKE ANY NECESSARY CHANGES BEFORE MOVING ON TO THE NEXT STEP OF CREATING YOUR COMIC BOOK.

IT IS NOT DIFFICULT TO MAKE A STORYBOARD. LOOK AT THE EXAMPLE ON THE NEXT PAGE.

WOW!

STORY BOARD EXAMPLE:

ORGANIZE YOUR STORY PLAN IN THESE PANELS AND, ADD NOTES

THE STORY TAKES PLACE AT SEA...

WE ARRIVE AT AN ISLAND WITH AN ACTIVE VOLCANO!

THE ISLAND HAS TONS OF AMAZING DINOSAURS...WHY AREN'T THEY EXTINCT?

OH NO! THE VOLCANO IS GOING TO EXPLODE!

WE RESCUE A DINOSAUR AND BRING HIM HOME WITH US!

OH NO, I DON'T KNOW HOW TO DRAW A CHARACTER... DO I NEED TO BE GOOD AT DRAWING?
??????
ART? NO PROBLEM, YOU DON'T NEED TO BE GOOD AT DRAWING TO MAKE A FUN COMIC
YOU CAN FOLLOW ALONG THE EXAMPLES OVER THE NEXT FEW PAGES. YOUR DRAWING STYLE IS WHAT ACTUALLY MAKES YOUR COMIC OR GRAPHIC NOVEL FUN AND INTERESTING. DON'T BE AFRAID TO BE CREATIVE AND TRY NEW THINGS.

I CAN'T DRAW!! HELP!
I CAN'T DRAW EITHER!
I ALSO DON'T KNOW IF I AM GOOD AT DRAWING

DON'T WORRY, FRIENDS! ANYONE CAN LEARN TO DRAW
WOOO HOO! I AM EXCITED!

Panel 1:
- "HI FOLKS!"
- "JIM DO YOU WORKOUT?"
- "JIM LOOKS GOOD..."

Panel 2:
- "JIM, WHAT'S YOUR SECRET?"
- "JUST FLEW BACK FROM FLORIDA"

Panel 3:
- "FLORIDA... MAYBE NEXT WINTER"

KEEP YOUR COMIC ART SIMPLE, AND EASY TO DRAW. TRY TO THINK OF AN INTERESTING STORY AND DIALOGUE FOR YOUR CHARACTERS.

STICK FIGURES!

- STICK FIGURE DRAWINGS ARE A COMMON FEATURE IN COMIC BOOKS.
- ANYONE CAN DRAW A STICK FIGURE, AND THEY ARE A GREAT WAY TO CONVEY IDEAS AND TELL STORIES WITHOUT REQUIRING ADVANCED DRAWING SKILLS.

YOU DON'T NEED A LOT OF ARTISTIC TALENT TO DRAW A COMIC, THE TRUTH IS THAT ANYONE CAN CREATE AN INTERESTING COMIC USING STICK FIGURES.

MANY POPULAR COMIC STRIPS AND WEBCOMICS FEATURE STICK FIGURES, AND THEY'VE PROVEN TO BE VERY POPULAR WITH READERS OF ALL AGES. BY USING SIMPLE LINES AND SHAPES TO CREATE CHARACTERS AND BACKGROUNDS, ARTISTS CAN FOCUS ON DEVELOPING THEIR STORYTELLING ABILITIES AND INTERESTING PLOTLINES.

STICK FIGURE DRAWINGS CAN HELP YOU BE MORE CREATIVE WITH YOUR STORY.

> TRY DRAWING YOURSELF AS A STICK FIGURE. HERE ARE SOME EXAMPLES BELOW. YOU CAN ADD SOME INTERESTING DESIGN ELEMENTS TO PERSONALIZE YOUR DRAWING. DO YOU WEAR GLASSES? HOW DO YOU WEAR YOUR HAIR? WHAT DO YOU LIKE TO WEAR?

HEY THERE!
I AM A STICK FIGURE.
CAN YOU DRAW
YOURSELF IN THIS
STYLE?

NOW YOU TRY IT!

TRY DRAWING YOUR FIGURE IN DIFFERENT POSES:

ONE DAY AT THE PARK...
Hi JERRY, HOW ARE YOU?
I AM SO BORED SAM...
MAYBE WE CAN DO SOMETHING?
JERRY, WHAT COULD WE DO?
MAYBE A TRIP? WHAT DOES THIS MAP SAY..
AS LONG AS MY DOG CAN COME
A TRiP TO THE DOG PARK? WE CAN USE THE GPS iN MY PHONE!
WOOF, WOOF

ACTION POSES

NOW YOU TRY IT!

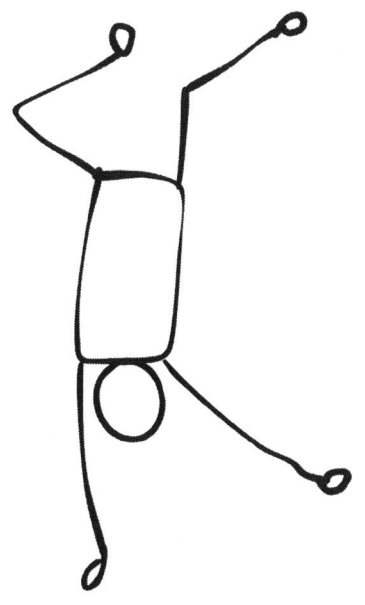

CREATING DYNAMIC ACTION POSES IS A GREAT WAY TO BRING YOUR CHARACTER TO LIFE AND ADD EXCITEMENT TO YOUR COMIC. CONSIDER THE MOVEMENTS OF YOUR CHARACTER: DO THEY JUMP, DANCE, OR KICK? TRY DRAWING A STICK FIGURE IN A KICKING POSE TO GET STARTED.

HERE ARE SOME MORE TIPS FOR YOUR COMIC:

- DEVELOP WELL-ROUNDED CHARACTERS WITH DISTINCT PERSONALITIES AND MOTIVATIONS.

- USE PACING TO CONTROL THE FLOW OF THE STORY AND KEEP READERS ENGAGED (BY FINDING THE RIGHT BALANCE BETWEEN ACTION AND EVENTS, WRITERS CAN CREATE AN ENGAGING STORY FROM BEGINNING TO END).

- USE A MIX OF DIALOGUE (SPEECH BUBBLES), NARRATION, AND VISUALS TO CONVEY THE STORY.

- ADD SOUND EFFECTS TO ENHANCE YOUR STORY.

- INCORPORATE INTERESTING AND UNIQUE SETTINGS AND VISUALS TO CREATE A MEMORABLE WORLD.

- STAY TRUE TO YOUR VISION. REMEMBER, THIS IS YOUR COMIC AND YOUR STORY!

- TAKE RISKS AND BE CREATIVE.

> MAKE SURE TO BALANCE THE AMOUNT OF DIALOGUE AND ACTION IN EACH PANEL. FOCUS ON THE STORY AND KEEP YOUR ART SIMPLE.

> PACING REFERS TO THE RHYTHM OF THE STORY AND HOW EVENTS FALL INTO PLACE. IT'S NOT NECESSARILY THE SPEED AT WHICH THE STORY IS TOLD, BUT MORE HOW FAST OR SLOW THE STORY IS MOVING FOR THE READER.

SUPER SIMPLE CHARACTER DESIGN:

> YOU CAN DRAW A SIMPLE CIRCULAR SHAPE, ADD SOME EYES, NOSE, MOUTH TO MAKE THIS FUN AND SIMPLE CHARACTER

CONFUSED

SAYING HELLO

ELECTROCUTED

SAD

DISAPPOINTED

HAPPY

> DON'T OVER-DESIGN YOUR CHARACTERS AS YOU WOULD NEED TO DRAW THEM MANY TIMES THROUGHOUT YOUR COMIC BOOK (30 TIMES? 100 TIMES?). REMEMBER TO KEEP YOUR DESIGN SIMPLE, FUN, AND EASY TO DRAW.

MINI COMIC IDEA: DRAW A SIMPLE CHARACTER, AND COME UP WITH A FUNNY STORY.

DRAW A SIMPLE BLOB, ADD SOME EYES AND A MOUTH...

MAIN CHARACTER: BOB THE BLOB

HERE IS AN EXAMPLE:

EVENT: LOOKING FOR STEVE?

Panel 1: STEVE? / I AM NOT STEVE

Panel 2: I AM BOB, WHO IS THIS STEVE?

Panel 3: I AM ALSO BOB

Panel 4: STEVE...

Panel 5: SO...WHERE IS STEVE?

Panel 6: STEVE, ARE YOU THERE?

Panel 7: STEVE?

Panel 8: ARE YOU TALKING ABOUT ME?

SUPER CAT

I AM SUPER CAT!!

MEOW!!

UP, UP AND AWAY!!

WHAT ARE YOU THINKING?

HI THERE!

MAIN CHARACTER: SUPER CAT
POWERS: FLYING AND MIND READING
LOVES: CAT FOOD AND TREATS
GOAL: WANTS TO SAVE THE WORLD
HATES: ANGRY DOGS, BARKING AND LOUD NOISES!

SUPER PUP

"I AM SUPER PUP!"

FLYING POWERS!

SUPER-SONIC BARK

BARK BARK

SMELLY PEE POWER!

STINKY BREATH?

DIGGING POWER??

PUP-FU!

DRAW YOUR CHARACTER IN DIFFERENT POSES AND WITH DIFFERENT EXPRESSIONS. YOU CAN LATER USE THIS CHARACTER IN YOUR COMIC. THIS WOULD GIVE YOU AN IDEA FOR HOW THIS CHARACTER MOVES, LOOKS AND BEHAVES.

SUPER PUP RESCUE! CAN YOU FILL THE REST OF THESE PANELS? WHOM DOES SUPER PUP RESCUE?

I AM SUPER PUP! WHO NEEDS A RESCUE?

WHEN YOU'RE FIRST STARTING OUT, IT'S EASY TO GET OVERWHELMED WITH DETAILS. KEEP YOUR STORY AND ARTWORK SIMPLE. FOCUS ON THE MOST IMPORTANT PARTS OF YOUR STORY.

MAKING MISTAKES IS A NATURAL PART OF THE CREATIVE PROCESS. DON'T WORRY IF YOUR FIRST ATTEMPTS AREN'T PERFECT.

DID YOU KNOW?

- THE PROCESS OF CREATING A COMIC BOOK BEGINS WITH A SCRIPT THAT OUTLINES THE STORY, FOLLOWED BY THE ARTIST SKETCHING ROUGH LAYOUTS KNOWN AS "THUMBNAILS."
    - ARTISTS USE VARIOUS TECHNIQUES TO BRING CHARACTERS TO LIFE, INCLUDING PENCILING (CREATING THE INITIAL DRAWINGS), INKING (ADDING DARK OUTLINES AND DETAILS), AND COLORING (ADDING VIBRANT HUES).

- MANY COMIC BOOK ARTISTS HAVE UNIQUE SIGNATURE STYLES THAT MAKE THEIR WORK INSTANTLY RECOGNIZABLE.
    - COMIC BOOK CONVENTIONS, LIKE COMIC-CON INTERNATIONAL, BRING TOGETHER FANS, ARTISTS, WRITERS, AND PUBLISHERS TO CELEBRATE AND SHOWCASE THE WORLD OF COMICS, OFFERING OPPORTUNITIES FOR CREATORS TO INTERACT WITH THEIR AUDIENCE.

- THE TERM "SUPERHERO" GOES AS FAR BACK AS 1899. AROUND 1917 IT BECOME MORE POPULAR AND WAS USED TO DESCRIBE CHARACTERS WITH EXTRAORDINARY ABILITIES AND HEROIC QUALITIES (SUCH AS ROBIN HOOD).
    - IN 1936, LEE FALK, INVENTED THE FIRST SUPERHERO, THE PHANTOM, WHO HAD HIS OWN NEWSPAPER COMIC STRIP.
    - IN 1938, DC COMICS INTRODUCED SUPERMAN. WRITER JERRY SIEGEL AND ARTIST JOE SHUSTER, HAD UNSUCCESSFULLY TRIED TO SELL THE SERIES TO NEWSPAPER SYNDICATES AS A DAILY STRIP. THROUGHOUT THE 1940S AND 1950S, SUPERMAN WAS THE MOST POPULAR COMIC BOOK CHARACTER. HIS POWERS ALSO GREW AS HE GREW IN POPULARITY.

CAN YOU DRAW THE NEXT PANELS? HOW DOES THE STORY CONTINUE?

ALIEN INVASION!

HOW DOES THE ALIEN INVASION STORY END?
CAN YOU THINK OF AN INTERESTING ENDING?

SHAPE, COLOR AND SILHOUETTE

SILHOUETTE: THE SILHOUETTE OF A CHARACTER IS ITS OVERALL SHAPE, AND IT'S IMPORTANT TO CREATE A DISTINCTIVE AND RECOGNIZABLE SHAPE FOR EACH CHARACTER.

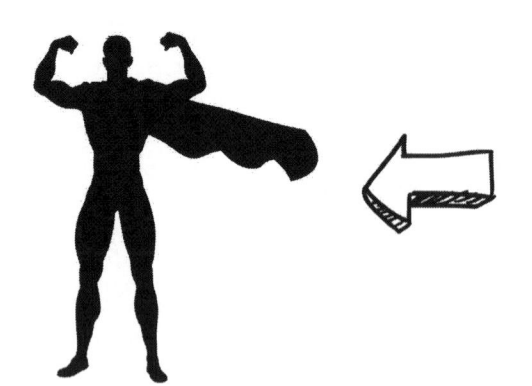

A STRONG SILHOUETTE CAN HELP A CHARACTER STAND OUT AND BE EASILY IDENTIFIABLE

SHAPE: THE SHAPE PF YOUR CHARACTER'S BODY PARTS, HEAD, ARMS, AND LEGS, CAN TELL A LOT ABOUT THEIR PERSONALITY AND ACTIONS.

- BROAD SHOULDERS CAN INDICATE STRENGTH AND CONFIDENCE.
- ROUND SHAPES CONVEY A CUTE AND FRIENDLY PERSONALITY.

COLOR OF A CHARACTER'S OUTFIT AND OVERALL COLOR SCHEME CAN ALSO TELL US A LOT ABOUT THEIR PERSONALITY AND ACTIONS.

- BRIGHT COLORS MIGHT SUGGEST A HAPPY OR ENERGETIC PERSONALITY.
- HOWEVER, DARK COLORS MIGHT SUGGEST A MORE BROODING OR SERIOUS DEMEANOR.

SUPERMAN'S RED AND BLUE COLORS ARE BRIGHT AND STRONG, AND HIS RED CAPE IS VERY EASY TO RECOGNIZE. HE HAS A STRONG SQUARED JAW WITH BROAD SHOULDERS. WE CAN TELL HE IS A HERO AND FIGHTS FOR GOOD.

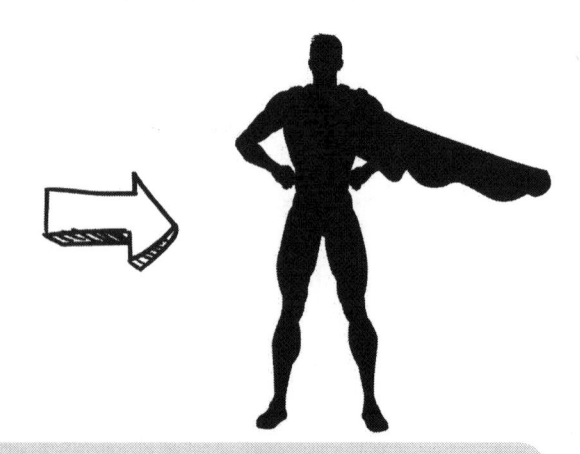

A STRONG SILHOUETTE HELPS YOUR CHARACTER STAND OUT AGAINST OTHER CHARACTERS IN THE STORY. IT ALSO MAKES IT EASY TO SPOT EVEN IN SMALL PANELS.

BODY AND FACIAL EXPRESSIONS

THE PROPORTIONS OF A CHARACTER'S BODY PARTS SHOULD BE CONSISTENT.
- CONSIDER YOUR CHARACTER'S AGE, GENDER, AND PHYSICAL ABILITIES.

> BODY LANGUAGE AND FACIAL EXPRESSIONS ARE VERY POWERFUL WHEN ESTABLISHING A CHARACTER'S EMOTIONS AND INNER FEELINGS, IN WAYS WORDS CAN NOT. ALSO CONSIDER ADDING SYMBOLS OR ACCESSORIES (GLASSES? LASER BEAM? SWORD?)

FACIAL EXPRESSIONS CAN CONVEY A LOT ABOUT THE EMOTIONS AND PERSONALITY OF YOUR CHARACTER. PRACTICE CREATING A RANGE OF FACIAL EXPRESSIONS THAT ARE CONSISTENT WITH THE CHARACTER'S PERSONALITY AND THE TONE OF THE STORY. IT DOESN'T HAVE TO BE VERY COMPLEX, HERE IS AN EXAMPLE:

CAN YOU IDENTIFY THESE EMOTIONS?

SAD?
HAPPY?
DISGUSTED?
CONFUSED?
SURPRISED?
CONFIDENT?

SHAPE LANGUAGE

WHEN CREATING A COMIC BOOK CHARACTER, SHAPES ARE IMPORTANT BECAUSE THEY CAN CONVEY DIFFERENT EMOTIONS AND PERSONALITIES.

> SHAPE LANGUAGE IN CHARACTER DESIGN INVOLVES USING DIFFERENT SHAPES, LINES, AND FORMS TO COMMUNICATE SPECIFIC ATTRIBUTES OR EMOTIONS RELATED TO THE CHARACTER'S PERSONALITY, VALUES, AND MOTIVATIONS.

ANGULAR AND SHARP SHAPES CAN INDICATE AGGRESSION OR DANGER, WHILE SOFT AND ROUNDED SHAPES CAN CONVEY A MORE GENTLE OR APPROACHABLE CHARACTER. THICK AND BULKY SHAPES SUGGEST STRENGTH, WHILE THIN AND DELICATE SHAPES INDICATE FRAGILITY. CONSISTENT USE OF SHAPE LANGUAGE THROUGHOUT THE CHARACTER'S DESIGN CREATES A COHERENT AND MEMORABLE VISUAL IDENTITY.

SHAPES CAN HELP DEFINE YOUR CHARACTER'S PHYSICAL FEATURES AND DISTINGUISH THEM FROM OTHER CHARACTERS IN THE STORY. THEY ALSO HELP CONVEY EMOTIONS AND GIVE YOUR CHARACTER AN INTERESTING PERSONALITY.

THE THREE MOST COMMON SHAPES USED IN COMICS ARE: CIRCLES, SQUARES AND TRIANGLES.

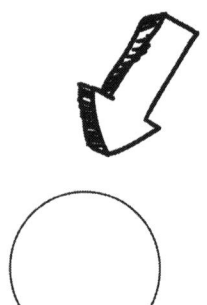

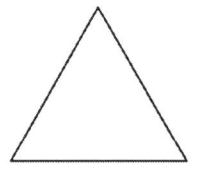

Shape language is an essential tool used in comic book creation to convey meaning and emotions to readers. Different shapes can evoke specific emotions, and understanding their meanings is vital to effective storytelling. Here are the three most common shapes used in comics and their significance:

- **Circles:** Circles represent completeness, and balance. They can convey feelings of harmony, happiness, and even eternity. In comics, circles are used to show a character's positive emotions or state of mind. For example, a character may have a circular speech bubble when they are feeling happy or content.

- **Squares:** Squares symbolize stability, order, and rationality. They are often used to represent buildings, objects, or environments that are reliable and steady. In comics, squares can be used to show a character's logical thinking or analytical mindset. For instance, a character who is calculating their next move might have a square thought bubble.

- **Triangles:** Triangles represent tension, conflict, and drama. They are often used in action scenes to convey a sense of danger or urgency. In comics, triangles can be used to depict a villain or a character who is causing trouble. For example, a villain might have a triangular speech bubble or a pointed hairstyle to signify their evil intentions.

Understanding the significance of circles, squares, and triangles helps artists and writers create interesting stories and characters.

WORD ASSOCIATIONS WITH SHAPES:

SQUARE

SOLID
STRONG
BALANCED
RELIABLE
NOT FLEXIBLE
STURDY
GOOD

CIRCLE

CUTE
FRIENDLY
SOFT
NICE
SWEET
APPROACHABLE
PEACEFUL

TRIANGLE

DYNAMIC
SHARP
FAST
DANGEROUS
DIRECTIONAL
UNPREDICTABLE
SMART

ANGULAR SHAPES MAY APPEAR MORE AGGRESSIVE OR INTIMIDATING, WHILE A CHARACTER WITH SOFTER, ROUNDER SHAPES MAY APPEAR MORE APPROACHABLE OR FRIENDLY. SQUARED SHAPES APPEAR STRONG.

DRAW DIFFERENT EXPRESSIONS BELOW:
- TAKE A LOOK AT THESE FACIAL OUTLINES, WHO LOOKS LIKE A HERO AND WHO LOOKS LIKE A VILLAIN?

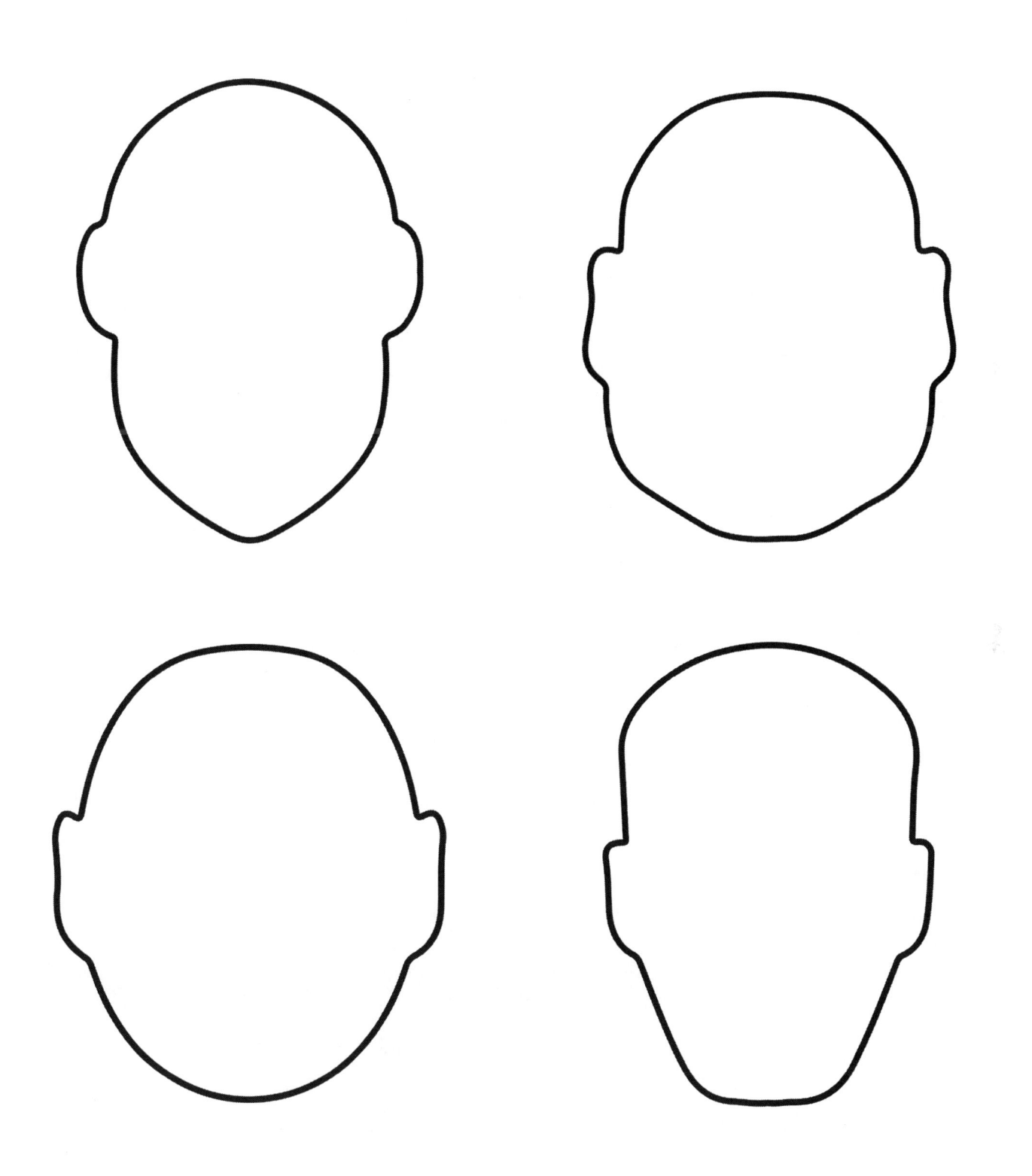

DID YOU KNOW?

- BATMAN IS A CHARACTER WHO EMBODIES SQUARES AND TRIANGLES IN HIS DESIGN. HIS COSTUME, INCLUDING HIS EMBLEM, COWL, AND CAPE, ARE ALL SQUARE-SHAPED! HIS LOOK REPRESENTS HIS RATIONAL AND ANALYTICAL MINDSET AS WELL AS HIS RELIANCE ON GADGETS. THE TRIANGLES ON HIS EARS AND CAPE ADD A SENSE OF TENSION. BATMAN IS DRESSED IN BLACK AND REPRESENTS DANGER TO CRIMINALS.

- SUPERMAN, ON THE OTHER HAND, HAS CIRCLES AND SQUARES IN HIS DESIGN. HIS ICONIC "S" EMBLEM, ROUNDED MUSCLES, SQUARED JAW AND FLOWING CAPE ALL CONVEY A SENSE OF HARMONY AND HOPE. THE CIRCULAR SHAPE OF HIS SYMBOL EMPHASIZES HIS HERO STATUS, AS IT RESEMBLES A SHIELD.

- THE JOKER HAS A DESIGN THAT INCORPORATES BOTH CIRCLES AND TRIANGLES. HE IS CHAOTIC! HIS SMILE AND EYES ARE CIRCULAR, WHICH CAN REPRESENT HAPPINESS AND JOY, BUT IN THE CONTEXT OF HIS TWISTED AND VIOLENT BEHAVIOR, THEY BECOME CREEPY... THE JAGGED EDGES AND SHARP ANGLES OF HIS SUIT AND HAIR ADD A SENSE OF DANGER AND UNPREDICTABILITY.

- SPIDER-MAN CHARACTER DESIGN IS INFLUENCED BY CIRCLES, WHICH REPRESENT HIS AGILITY AND FLEXIBILITY. THE CIRCULAR SHAPES ON HIS COSTUME, INCLUDING HIS WEBBING, EYES, AND SPIDER EMBLEM, ALL EMPHASIZE HIS SPEED AND FLEXIBILITY. THE USE OF CIRCLES ALSO MAKES HIM APPEAR MORE APPROACHABLE AND FRIENDLY. SPIDER-MAN IS KNOWN FOR HIS HUMOR AND WIT.

IF YOU COULD BE ANY SUPER HERO, WHO WOULD YOU LIKE TO BE AND WHY? WHAT POWERS WOULD YOU HAVE? HOW WOULD YOU USE YOUR POWERS? WHAT SHAPES WOULD YOU USE FOR YOUR CHARACTER DESIGN?

DESIGN ELEMENTS: DESIGN ELEMENTS LIKE ACCESSORIES, TATTOOS, AND SCARS CAN ADD DEPTH AND INTEREST TO YOUR CHARACTER'S APPEARANCE. HOWEVER, THEY SHOULD ALSO BE CONSISTENT WITH THE CHARACTER'S PERSONALITY AND BACKSTORY.

> WHAT DESIGN ELEMENTS COULD WE ADD TO MAKE THE CHARACTER MORE INTERESTING? GLASSES? A CAPE? MASK? GLOVES? BOOTS? SWORD?

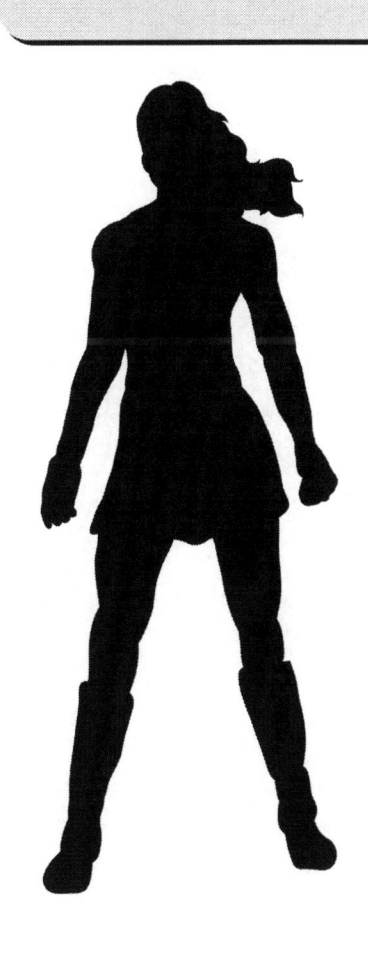

CONTEXT: THE CONTEXT OF THE STORY AND THE WORLD THE CHARACTER INHABITS SHOULD ALSO BE CONSIDERED WHEN DESIGNING A CHARACTER. A CHARACTER WHO LIVES IN A MEDIEVAL FANTASY WORLD WILL HAVE DIFFERENT CLOTHING, WEAPONS, AND OTHER DESIGN ELEMENTS THAN A CHARACTER WHO LIVES IN A FUTURISTIC SCI-FI SETTING.

MAKE SURE THAT YOUR DESIGN ELEMENTS FIT THE CONTEXT OF YOUR STORY.

PENCILING AND INKING

- PENCILING IS THE INITIAL STEP WHERE AN ARTIST USES A PENCIL TO CREATE THE ROUGH SKETCHES AND DRAWINGS OF THE ARTWORK. DURING THIS STAGE, THE ARTIST TYPICALLY WORKS ON LARGE SHEETS OF PAPER OR USES SPECIALIZED COMIC ART BOARDS. IN THIS STEP THE FOCUS IS ON CHARACTER DESIGN AND POSES, THE COMPOSITION OF THE PANEL AND SOME DETAILS FOR THE SCENES.
    - PENCILING INVOLVES CREATING THE BASIC SHAPES, LINES, AND OUTLINES, AND IT HELPS TO ESTABLISH THE OVERALL VISUAL FOR THE COMIC.

- ONCE THE PENCILING STAGE IS COMPLETE, THE NEXT STEP IS INKING. INKING INVOLVES GOING OVER THE PENCIL LINES WITH INK, ADDING WEIGHT, DEPTH, AND PRECISION TO THE ARTWORK.
    - THE INKING STAGE IS WHERE THE FINAL, POLISHED LINES ARE CREATED, GIVING THE ART A CLEAN AND PROFESSIONAL LOOK.
    - INKERS USE TOOLS, SUCH AS INK PENS, BRUSHES, OR EVEN DIGITAL SOFTWARE, TO TRACE OVER THE PENCIL LINES.

- INKING REFINES AND FINALIZES THE ARTWORK, GIVING IT A FINISHED AND PROFESSIONAL LOOK.

> REMEMBER, AS A COMIC CREATOR, YOUR FOCUS SHOULD BE ON ORGANIZING YOUR STORY FIRST AND YOUR ART (PENCILING AND INKING) SECOND.

TRY THIS IDEA (HERO DESIGN):

- CHOOSE A NAME FOR YOUR HERO:
    - CAPTAIN THUNDERBOLT

- CHOOSE A POWER OR ABILITY FOR YOUR HERO:
    - LIGHTNING CONTROL, CAN GENERATE ELECTRICITY!?

- CHOOSE A WEAKNESS OR VULNERABILITY FOR YOUR HERO:
    - VULNERABLE TO WATER

- CHOOSE A COSTUME OR UNIFORM FOR YOUR HERO:
    - BLUE AND YELLOW SUIT WITH LIGHTNING BOLT EMBLEM

- CREATE A BACKSTORY FOR YOUR HERO:
    - CAPTAIN THUNDERBOLT GAINED HIS POWERS AFTER BEING STRUCK BY LIGHTNING DURING A STORM. HE USES HIS POWERS TO FIGHT CRIME AND PROTECT HIS CITY FROM VILLAINS.

- CREATE A LIST OF ALLIES OR FRIENDS YOUR HERO HAS:
    - DETECTIVE ANNA, A POLICE OFFICER WHO WORKS WITH CAPTAIN THUNDERBOLT TO FIGHT CRIME.

- CREATE A LIST OF ENEMIES OR VILLAINS YOUR HERO FACES:
    - SHOCKWAVE, A VILLAIN WHO CAN CREATE EARTHQUAKES AND SHAKE THE GROUND. SHOCKWAVE WANTS TO TAKE OVER THE CITY!

- WRITE A BRIEF SUMMARY OF A TYPICAL ADVENTURE YOUR HERO MIGHT HAVE:
    - CAPTAIN THUNDERBOLT MUST STOP SHOCKWAVE FROM USING HIS POWERS TO ROB A BANK AND ESCAPE WITH THE MONEY. ANNA COMES IN TO INVESTIGATE, AND HELPS CAPTAIN THUNDERBOLT TRACK DOWN SHOCKWAVE! CAPTAIN THUNDERBOLT FIGHTS SHOCKWAVE AND USES HIS LIGHTNING POWERS TO SHORT-CIRCUIT HIS SUIT, DEFEATING HIM AND SAVING THE DAY.

NOW YOU TRY IT:

- CHOOSE A NAME FOR YOUR HERO:

___

- CHOOSE A POWER OR ABILITY FOR YOUR HERO:

___

- CHOOSE A WEAKNESS OR VULNERABILITY FOR YOUR HERO:

___

- CHOOSE A COSTUME OR UNIFORM FOR YOUR HERO:

___

- CREATE A BACKSTORY FOR YOUR HERO:

___

- CREATE A LIST OF ALLIES OR FRIENDS YOUR HERO HAS:

___

- CREATE A LIST OF ENEMIES OR VILLAINS YOUR HERO FACES:

___

- WRITE A BRIEF SUMMARY OF A TYPICAL ADVENTURE YOUR HERO MIGHT HAVE:

___

WHAT DOES YOUR HERO LOOK LIKE?

DRAW YOUR HERO BELOW! TRY DRAWING YOUR HERO STANDING AND SITTING, MAYBE DRAW A SIDE VIEW?

SUBMERGE-O

NAME: SUBMERGE-O THE OCTOPUS SUPERHERO

POWERS:
- **OCTOPUS POWER:** HE CAN STRETCH HIS ARMS AND TENTACLES IN ALL DIRECTIONS, MAKING HIM INCREDIBLY FLEXIBLE. WHETHER HE NEEDS TO REACH FOR SOMETHING FAR AWAY OR GIVE A GROUP OF VILLAINS A GROUP HUG!

- **SHARK SPEED:** HE CAN ZIP THROUGH THE WATER WITH LIGHTNING-FAST AGILITY. HE'S THE SPEEDIEST SWIMMER IN THE SEA AND OFTEN PLAYS TAG WITH DOLPHINS!

ABILITIES:
AS A MASTER OF DIVING, SUBMERGE-O CAN EXPLORE THE DEPTHS OF THE OCEAN LIKE NO OTHER. HE CAN WITHSTAND TREMENDOUS WATER PRESSURE AND EVEN TALK WITH MARINE CREATURES (MOSTLY FISH, DOLPHINS, TURTLES AND WHALES.. JELLY FISH ARE HARDER TO UNDERSTAND FOR SOME REASON...).

APPEARANCE:
A SHINY SILVER WETSUIT, HIS ARMS AND FEET CAN TRANSFORM INTO OCTOPUS TENTACLES. HE HAS A STREAMLINED HELMET. HIS OUTFIT HELPS HIM DIVE DEEPER THAN ANY HUMAN.

PERSONALITY:
SUBMERGE-O LOVES CRACKING JOKES, ESPECIALLY PUNS RELATED TO THE SEA. HE'S ALWAYS READY TO LEND A HELPING TENTACLE AND HAS A KNACK FOR TURNING TENSE SITUATIONS INTO LAUGHTER-FILLED MOMENTS.

CATCHPHRASE:
"TIME TO DIVE INTO ACTION AND SOAK UP THE FUN!"

ARCH-NEMESIS:
CAPTAIN POLLUTION, AN EVIL VILLAIN WHO'S DETERMINED TO POLLUTE THE OCEANS AND DESTROY MARINE LIFE. SUBMERGE-O'S MISSION IS TO STOP CAPTAIN POLLUTION'S DESTRUCTIVE PLANS AND PROTECT THE UNDERWATER WORLD.

STORY:
SUBMERGE-O HAS TO RESCUES A GROUP OF STRANDED SAILORS AND UNCOVERS ANCIENT SUNKEN TREASURES. HE MUST ALSO STOP CAPTAIN POLLUTION'S DIABOLICAL SCHEMES. REMEMBER, WITH SUBMERGE-O AROUND, THE OCEAN'S DEPTHS WILL NEVER BE DULL!

WHAT SHOULD SUBMERGE-O LOOK LIKE? WOULD HE HAVE TENTACLES OR A SPECIAL DESIGN ON HIS SUIT? WOULD YOU HE BE MORE MAN OR MORE OCTOPUS?

CAN YOU COME UP WITH A DESIGN FOR SUBMERGE-O

IDEAS

THE NEXT FEW PAGES ARE IDEA PAGES. THESE SHOULD HELP YOU OUT ON YOUR COMIC BOOK JOURNEY! GOOD LUCK!

HERO IDEAS...

- **CAPTAIN JUMBLE:** WITH THE POWER TO SCRAMBLE ANY PUZZLE OR RIDDLE, CAPTAIN JUMBLE LEAVES VILLAINS SCRATCHING THEIR HEADS IN CONFUSION.

- **THE MIGHTY MUNCHER:** ARMED WITH AN INSATIABLE APPETITE, THE MIGHTY MUNCHER DEVOURS ANYTHING IN SIGHT AND CAN REGURGITATE USEFUL ITEMS WHEN NEEDED (DISGUSTING!).

- **THE ELASTIC TICKLER:** USING THEIR STRETCHY LIMBS AND TICKLING PROWESS, THIS HERO DISARMS ENEMIES WITH TICKLES!

- **SUPER SNIFFER:** POSSESSING AN EXTRAORDINARY SENSE OF SMELL, SUPER SNIFFER CAN DETECT EVEN THE FAINTEST ODORS TO TRACK DOWN ENEMIES AND STOP EVIL PLANS.

- **CAPTAIN CLUMSY:** WITH AMPLIFIED CLUMSINESS, CAPTAIN CLUMSY UNINTENTIONALLY TRIUMPHS OVER VILLAINS, LEAVING THEM DEFEATED AND LAUGHING AT THEIR OWN MISHAPS.

- **THE DAZZLING DOODLE:** THIS ARTISTIC HERO BRINGS THEIR DRAWINGS TO LIFE, USING THEM AS ALLIES AND TOOLS TO OUTSMART ENEMIES.

- **THE BUBBLE BLASTER:** CREATING BUBBLES OF ALL SHAPES AND SIZES, THIS HERO DEPLOYS PROTECTIVE SHIELDS AND SLIPPERY TRAPS TO IMMOBILIZE VILLAINS.

- **THE MEGA MAGNET:** CONTROLLING MAGNETISM, THIS HERO ATTRACTS OR REPELS OBJECTS AT WILL, CAUSING CHAOS OR RESTORING ORDER AS NEEDED.

- **THE GIGGLING GHOST:** A MISCHIEVOUS SPIRIT THAT POSSESSES OBJECTS, THE GIGGLING GHOST PLAYS TRICKS ON VILLAINS AND UNSUSPECTING HEROES, LEAVING THEM IN FITS OF LAUGHTER.

- **THE HYPNOTIST:** SHE IS ARMED WITH A SWINGING POCKET WATCH. SHE MESMERIZES VILLAINS WITH HER EYES AND HYPNOTIC LAUGHTER, RENDERING THEM HELPLESS.

NOW YOU TRY IT! WHO IS YOUR HERO?

FUNNY STORY PROMPTS...

A HERO WHO CAN FLY, BUT GETS TERRIBLE MOTION SICKNESS AND ALWAYS THROWS UP MID-FLIGHT. (DUSGUSTING!)	A VILLAIN WHO'S ALWAYS LATE TO THEIR OWN EVIL PLANS BECAUSE THEY SPEND TOO MUCH TIME DECIDING WHAT OUTFIT TO WEAR.	A SIDEKICK WHO'S ALLERGIC TO THEIR OWN POWERS AND BREAKS OUT IN HIVES EVERY TIME THEY USE THEM??
A SUPERHERO WHO CAN TURN INVISIBLE, BUT IT DOESN'T ALWAYS WORK...	A SUPERHERO TEAM WHO ARE ALL SECRETLY AFRAID OF THEIR OWN POWERS AND SPEND MOST OF THEIR TIME TRYING TO CONVINCE EACH OTHER THAT THEY'RE NOT SCARED.	A SUPERHERO WHO HAS THE POWER TO TALK TO ANIMALS!!
A VILLAIN WHO TRIES TO TAKE OVER THE WORLD WITH THEIR ARMY OF KILLER ROBOTS, BUT THE ROBOTS KEEP MALFUNCTIONING AND DOING SILLY THINGS...	A SIDEKICK WHO WANTS TO BE A SUPER HERO! HOW CAN THEY TAKE OVER THE SPOTLIGHT? WHAT CAN THEY DO TO BECOME THE MAIN HERO?	A HERO WHO HAS THE POWER TO MAKE OTHERS LAUGH AND DANCE LIKE NOBODY'S WATCHING!

CAN YOU THINK OF SOMETHING INTERESTING AND TURN THAT INTO A STORY?

STORY IDEAS...

- YOUR FAVORITE SUPERHERO HAS LOST THEIR POWERS! HOW WILL THEY SAVE THE DAY WITHOUT THEIR SUPERHUMAN ABILITIES?

- AN ALIEN RACE HAS INVADED YOUR TOWN AND IT'S UP TO YOU TO STOP THEM! HOW CAN YOU SAVE THE PLANET??

- YOU WAKE UP ONE DAY TO DISCOVER YOU HAVE A SUPER POWER! WHAT CAN YOU DO WITH YOUR NEW ABILITY?

- A GROUP OF MISCHIEVOUS EVIL TROLLS HAVE STOLEN ALL THE COLOR FROM THE WORLD! CAN A HERO BRING IT BACK?

- YOUR PET SUDDENLY GAINS THE POWER OF SPEECH! AMAZING! WHAT ADVENTURES WILL YOU GO ON TOGETHER?

- A GROUP OF VILLAINS HAS TAKEN OVER THE CITY AND IT'S UP TO YOU TO STOP THEM! CAN YOU COME UP WITH A PLAN TO SAVE THE DAY?

- A TIME MACHINE HAS BEEN INVENTED AND YOU GET TO GO BACK IN TIME TO ANY PERIOD IN HISTORY! WHAT WILL YOU DISCOVER AND HOW WILL IT AFFECT THE FUTURE?

- AN EVIL SORCERER HAS CAST A SPELL ON YOUR TOWN, CAUSING EVERYONE TO FALL ASLEEP FOREVER! CAN YOU FIND A WAY TO BREAK THE SPELL AND SAVE YOUR FRIENDS AND FAMILY?

- YOU'VE STUMBLED UPON A PORTAL TO A PARALLEL DIMENSION! A WHOLE NEW WORLD IS WAITING TO BE EXPLORED. DO YOU THINK IT'S A FRIENDLY PLACE, OR ARE THERE ENEMIES LURKING? WHAT ACTIONS WOULD YOU TAKE?

MORE STORY IDEAS...

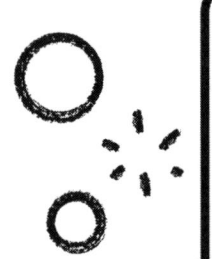

YOU DISCOVER A SECRET DOOR IN YOUR SCHOOL THAT LEADS TO A MYSTERIOUS UNDERGROUND LAB! WHAT EXPERIMENTS WILL YOU UNCOVER AND WHAT DANGERS WILL YOU FACE?

A SUPERHERO HAS LOST THEIR MEMORY AND FORGOTTEN WHO THEY ARE! CAN YOU AND YOUR FRIENDS HELP THEM REGAIN THEIR IDENTITY AND SAVE THE DAY?

A GROUP OF FAMOUS VILLAINS HAVE JOINED FORCES TO CREATE A SINISTER PLAN. CAN YOU AND YOUR FRIENDS STOP THEM BEFORE IT'S TOO LATE?

YOUR PET TURNED OUT TO BE AN EVIL ALIEN SPY! OH.. NO!! THERE IS A FULL ARMY COMING TO EARTH. CAN YOU SAVE THE WORLD?

YOUR BEST FRIEND GAINS A SUPER POWER, AND YOU BECOME THEIR SIDEKICK?? WHAT IS GOING ON!! CAN YOU SAVE THE WORLD TOGETHER?

YOUR TOWN IS BEING ATTACKED BY GIANT ROBOTS CONTROLLED BY A MAD SCIENTIST! CAN YOU AND YOUR FRIENDS CREATE YOUR OWN ROBOTS TO FIGHT BACK AND SAVE THE DAY?

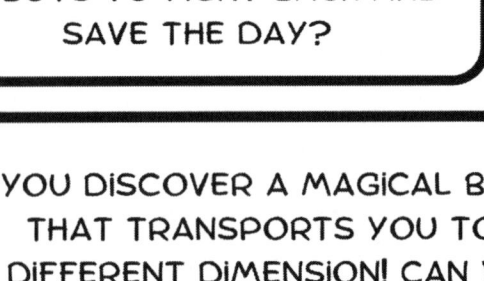

YOU FIND A MAP LEADING TO A TREASURE HIDDEN DEEP IN THE JUNGLE! CAN YOU NAVIGATE THROUGH THE DANGERS OF THE RAINFOREST TO FIND THE TREASURE?

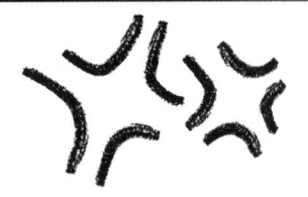

YOU DISCOVER A MAGICAL BOOK THAT TRANSPORTS YOU TO A DIFFERENT DIMENSION! CAN YOU FIND YOUR WAY BACK HOME BEFORE IT'S TOO LATE? CAN ANYONE HELP YOU ON YOUR MISSION??

HERE ARE SOME SPEECH BUBBLES
BOOM
YES!
WOW
THIS IS FUN
AWESOME!
YES!
WRITE THE TEXT AND ADD THE BUBBLE AROUND IT
YES!
TRY THESE IDEAS FOR YOUR SPEECH BUBBLES
AWESOME!
MAKE THE BUBBLE POINT TO THE HEAD OF YOUR CHARACTER
THIS IS COOL
YES
GREAT!
AWESOME!

IDEAS FOR YOUR CHARACTER!

GNOME	RABBIT	BAKER
SUPER VILLAIN	ALIEN	SUPER GRANDPA!
WITCH	SNOWMAN	SUPER COP

> IF YOU COULD BECOME A SUPER HERO, WHAT SUPER POWER WOULD YOU LIKE TO HAVE?

IDEAS FOR YOUR SETTING

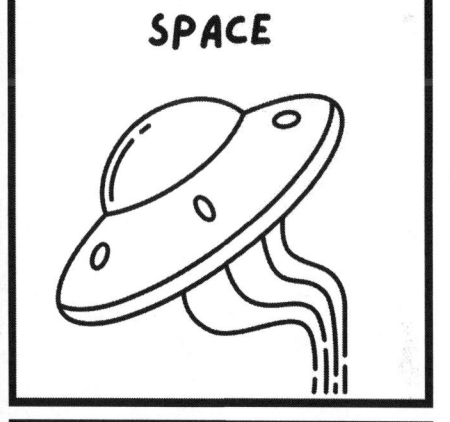

FARM	THE MOON	STORE
TOWN	UNDER THE SEA	SPACE
SCHOOL	CASTLE	FOREST

HERE ARE SOME ACTION WORDS TO HELP YOU MAKE A GREAT COMIC BOOK!

BOOM!

ZAP!

NO!

BOING!

OOPS!

ZONK

YES

BANG!

ZING

KA-POW!

SMASH!

BAM!

POW!

EEEK

HMMM

SNAP!

WOW!

POP!

TEMPLATES

THE TEMPLATES IN THIS BOOK ARE HERE TO HELP YOU CREATE YOUR OWN COMIC BOOK. THERE ARE A FEW IDEAS FOR YOU TO TRY AND EXPERIMENT WITH. HAVE FUN!

LET'S CREATE A STORY!

HERO	VILLAIN	SIDEKICK

SETTING	MAIN EVENT	ENDING

_____

_____

_____

_____

_____

_____

_____

LET'S CREATE A STORY!

HERO	VILLAIN	SIDEKICK

SETTING	MAIN EVENT	ENDING

_____

_____

_____

_____

_____

_____

_____

LET'S CREATE A STORY!

HERO	VILLAIN	SIDEKICK

SETTING	MAIN EVENT	ENDING

LET'S CREATE A STORY!

HERO	VILLAIN	SIDEKICK

SETTING	MAIN EVENT	ENDING

SIMPLE STORY TEMPLATE

HERO? VILLAIN? SIDEKICK?	WHERE DOES THE STORY TAKE PLACE?	WHAT HAPPENS? HOW DOES IT END?
CHARACTER	SETTING	EVENT

SIMPLE STORY TEMPLATE

HERO? VILLAIN? SIDEKICK?

| CHARACTER |

WHERE DOES THE STORY TAKE PLACE?

| SETTING |

WHAT HAPPENS? HOW DOES IT END?

| EVENT |

SIMPLE STORY TEMPLATE

HERO? VILLAIN? SIDEKICK?	WHERE DOES THE STORY TAKE PLACE?	WHAT HAPPENS? HOW DOES IT END?
CHARACTER	SETTING	EVENT

SIMPLE STORY TEMPLATE

HERO? VILLAIN? SIDEKICK?	WHERE DOES THE STORY TAKE PLACE?	WHAT HAPPENS? HOW DOES IT END?
CHARACTER	SETTING	EVENT

DESIGN A CHARACTER:

- NAME YOUR CHARACTER: _____

- WHAT DO THEY LOOK LIKE? _____
_____

- SUPER POWERS? ABILITIES? _____
_____

- PERSONALITY? _____
_____

- CREATE A BACKSTORY FOR YOUR CHARACTER:
_____
_____
_____

- WEAKNESSES: _____

- SIDEKICK: _____

- CREATE A LIST OF ENEMIES OR VILLAINS YOUR HERO FACES:
_____
_____
_____

- CATCHPHRASE: _____
_____

DRAW YOUR CHARACTER:

NAME:

POWERS:

_____
_____
_____

WEAKNESSES:

_____
_____
_____

DRAW THEIR SIDEKICK:

NAME:

DRAW THEIR ENEMY:

NAME:

DESIGN A CHARACTER:

- NAME YOUR CHARACTER: _____

- WHAT DO THEY LOOK LIKE? _____
  _____

- SUPER POWERS? ABILITIES? _____
  _____

- PERSONALITY? _____
  _____

- CREATE A BACKSTORY FOR YOUR CHARACTER:
  _____
  _____
  _____

- WEAKNESSES: _____

- SIDEKICK: _____

- CREATE A LIST OF ENEMIES OR VILLAINS YOUR HERO FACES:
  _____
  _____
  _____

- CATCHPHRASE: _____
  _____

DRAW YOUR CHARACTER:

NAME:

POWERS:

_____

_____

_____

WEAKNESSES:

_____

_____

_____

DRAW THEIR SIDEKICK:

NAME:

DRAW THEIR ENEMY:

NAME:

DESIGN A CHARACTER:

- NAME YOUR CHARACTER: _____

- WHAT DO THEY LOOK LIKE? _____
_____

- SUPER POWERS? ABILITIES? _____
_____

- PERSONALITY? _____
_____

- CREATE A BACKSTORY FOR YOUR CHARACTER:
_____
_____
_____

- WEAKNESSES: _____

- SIDEKICK: _____

- CREATE A LIST OF ENEMIES OR VILLAINS YOUR HERO FACES:
_____
_____
_____

- CATCHPHRASE: _____
_____

DRAW YOUR CHARACTER:

NAME:

POWERS:
_____
_____
_____

WEAKNESSES:
_____
_____
_____

DRAW THEIR SIDEKICK:

NAME:

DRAW THEIR ENEMY:

NAME:

DESIGN A CHARACTER:

- NAME YOUR CHARACTER: _____

- WHAT DO THEY LOOK LIKE? _____
_____

- SUPER POWERS? ABILITIES? _____
_____

- PERSONALITY? _____
_____

- CREATE A BACKSTORY FOR YOUR CHARACTER:
_____
_____
_____

- WEAKNESSES: _____

- SIDEKICK: _____

- CREATE A LIST OF ENEMIES OR VILLAINS YOUR HERO FACES:
_____
_____
_____

- CATCHPHRASE: _____
_____

DRAW YOUR CHARACTER:

NAME:

POWERS:
_____
_____
_____

WEAKNESSES:
_____
_____
_____

DRAW THEIR SIDEKICK:

NAME:

DRAW THEIR ENEMY:

NAME:

CREATE YOUR CHARACTER

NAME: _____

POWERS: _____

WEAKNESS: _____

SIDEKICK: _____

ENEMY: _____

GOAL: _____

DRAW YOUR CHARACTER

DRAW YOUR CHARACTER

CREATE YOUR CHARACTER

NAME: _____

POWERS: _____

WEAKNESS: _____

SIDEKICK: _____

ENEMY: _____

GOAL: _____

DRAW YOUR CHARACTER

DRAW YOUR CHARACTER

CREATE YOUR CHARACTER

NAME: _____

POWERS: _____

WEAKNESS: _____

SIDEKICK: _____

ENEMY: _____

GOAL: _____

DRAW YOUR CHARACTER

DRAW YOUR CHARACTER

CREATE YOUR CHARACTER

NAME: _____

POWERS: _____

WEAKNESS: _____

SIDEKICK: _____

ENEMY: _____

GOAL: _____

DRAW YOUR CHARACTER

DRAW YOUR CHARACTER

DRAW YOUR CHARACTER (PRACTICE PANELS)

DRAW YOUR CHARACTER (PRACTICE PANELS)

DRAW YOUR CHARACTER (PRACTICE PANELS)

DRAW YOUR CHARACTER (PRACTICE PANELS)

STORY BOARD TEMPLATE

STORY BOARD TEMPLATE

STORY BOARD TEMPLATE

STORY BOARD TEMPLATE

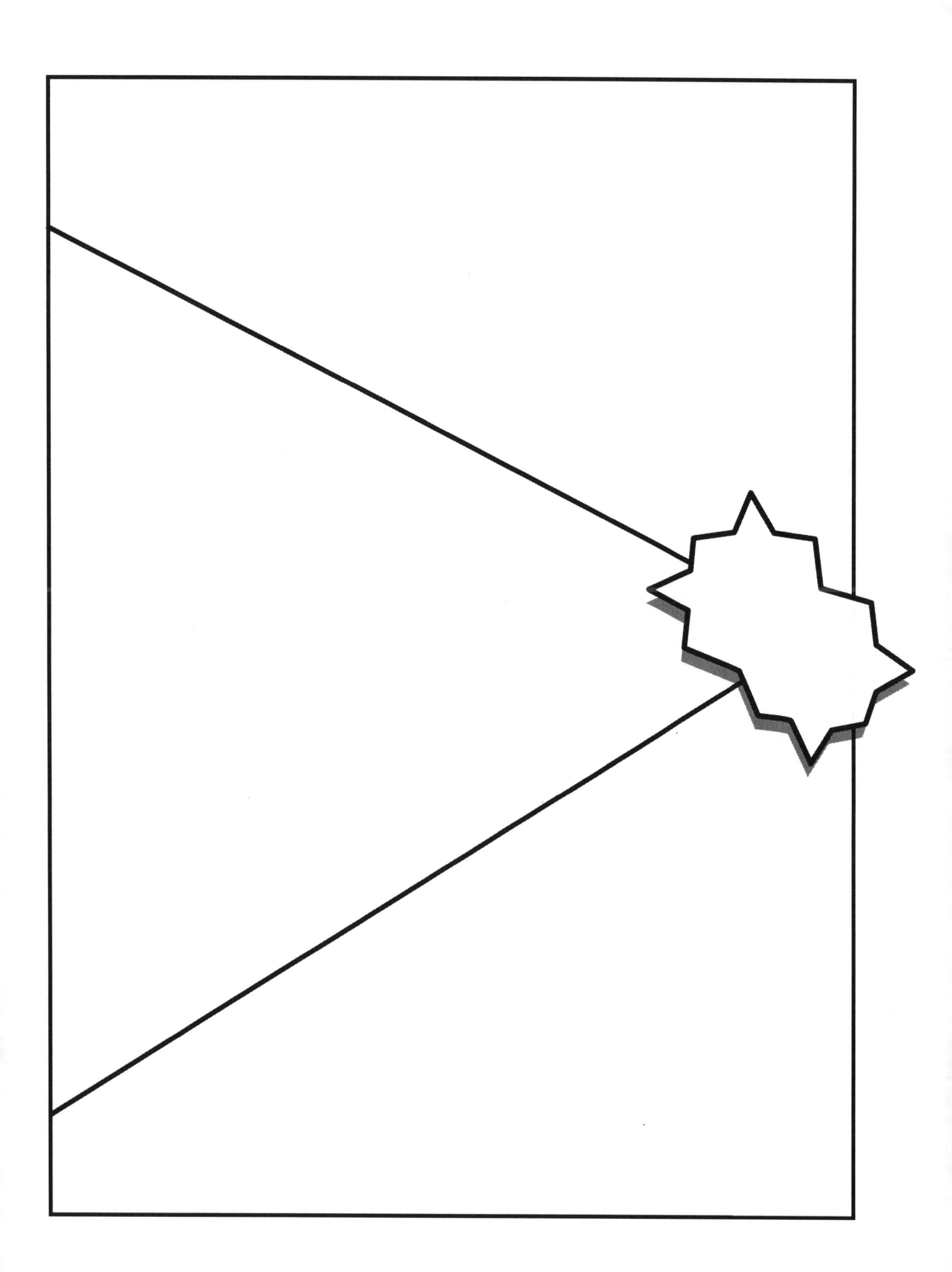

OOPS!

WOW!

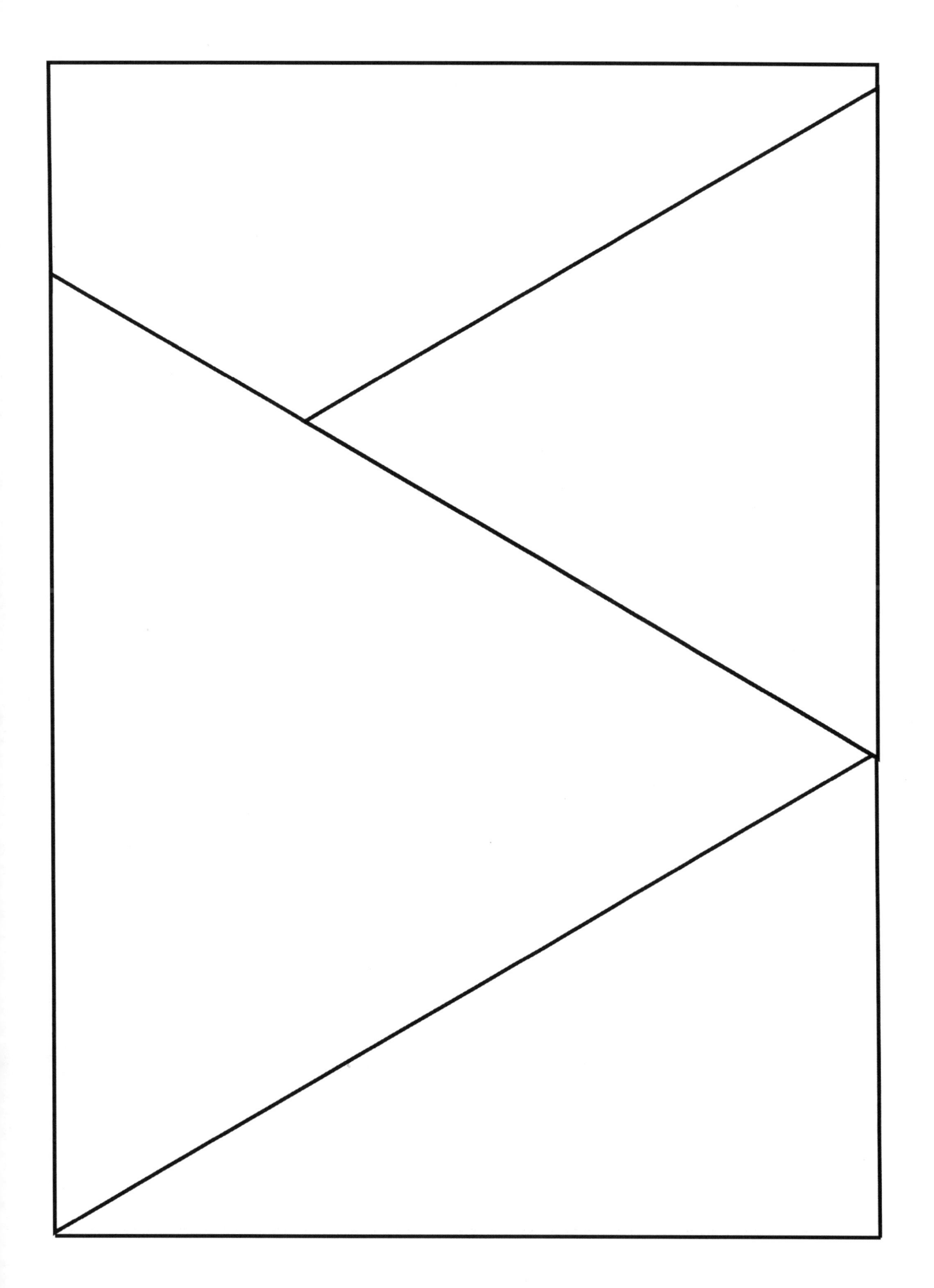

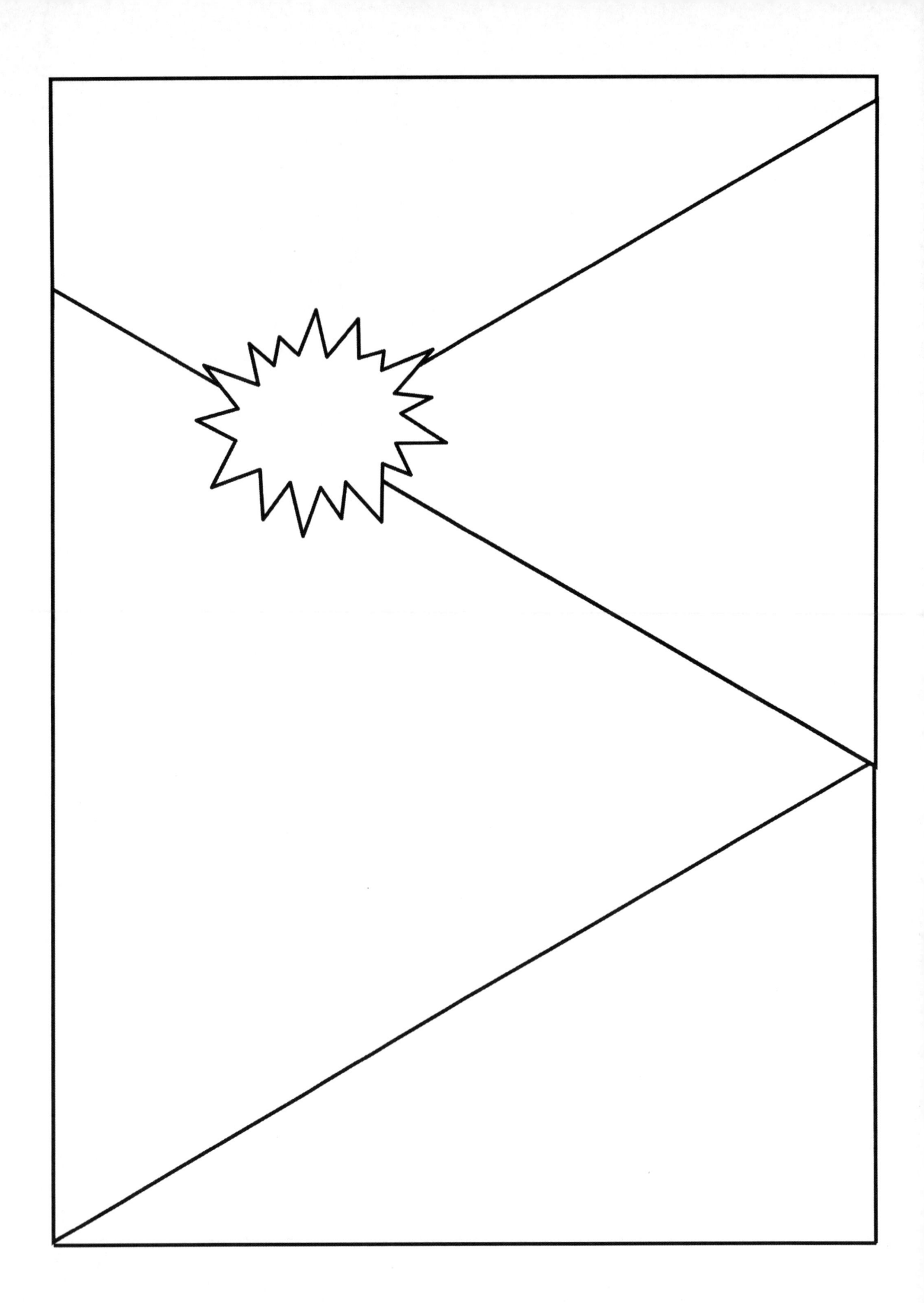

- PLAN OUT YOUR STORY
- PRACTICE DRAWING (DESIGN YOUR CHARACTERS AND DRAW THEM FROM DIFFERENT ANGLES AND IN DIFFERENT POSES)

- USE YOUR ARTWORK TO TELL YOUR STORY
- KEEP IT SIMPLE IF YOU ARE STARTING OUT
- DON'T BE AFRAID TO MAKE MISTAKES
- ASK FOR FEEDBACK

Printed in Great Britain
by Amazon